RIO GRANDE STEAM FINALE

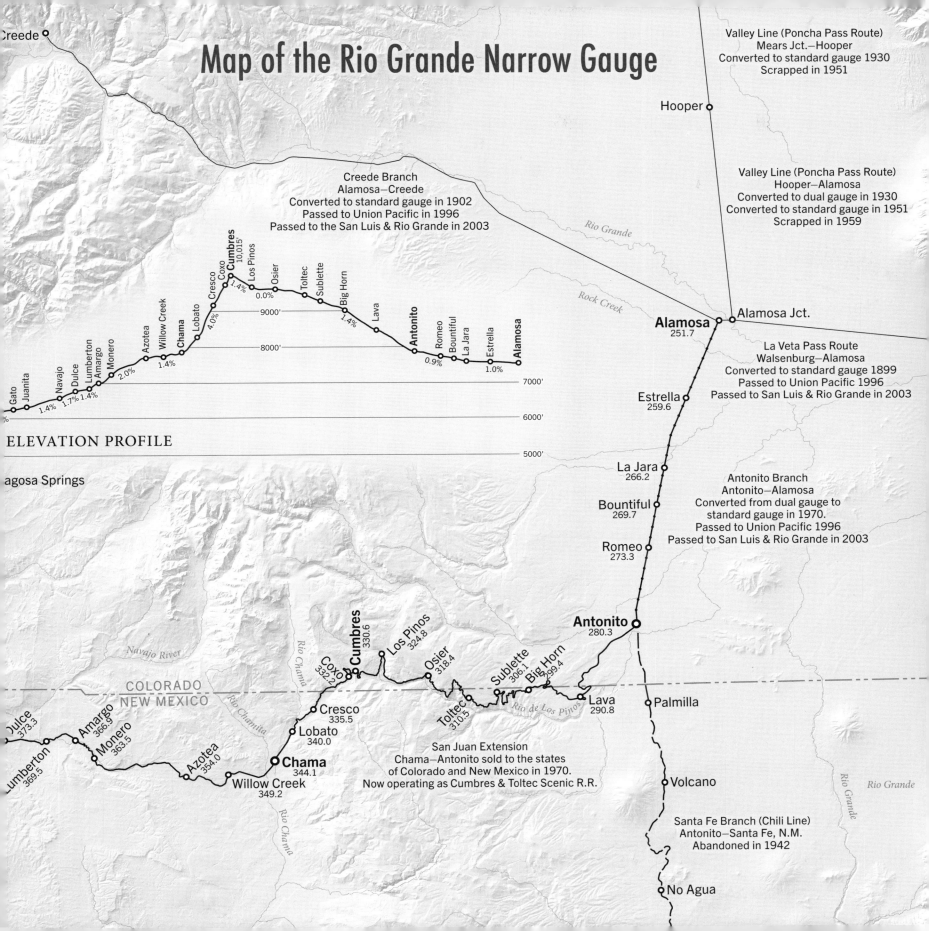

Map of the Rio Grande Narrow Gauge

Valley Line (Poncha Pass Route)
Mears Jct.–Hooper
Converted to standard gauge 1930
Scrapped in 1951

Hooper

Valley Line (Poncha Pass Route)
Hooper–Alamosa
Converted to dual gauge in 1930
Converted to standard gauge in 1951
Scrapped in 1959

Creede Branch
Alamosa–Creede
Converted to standard gauge in 1902
Passed to Union Pacific in 1996
Passed to the San Luis & Rio Grande in 2003

La Veta Pass Route
Walsenburg–Alamosa
Converted to standard gauge 1899
Passed to Union Pacific 1996
Passed to San Luis & Rio Grande in 2003

Antonito Branch
Antonito–Alamosa
Converted from dual gauge to
standard gauge in 1970.
Passed to Union Pacific 1996
Passed to San Luis & Rio Grande in 2003

San Juan Extension
Chama–Antonito sold to the states
of Colorado and New Mexico in 1970.
Now operating as Cumbres & Toltec Scenic R.R.

Santa Fe Branch (Chili Line)
Antonito–Santa Fe, N.M.
Abandoned in 1942

ELEVATION PROFILE

Cumbres 10,015'

Cumbres 1.4%
Coxo
Cresco 4.0%
Los Pinos 0.0%
Osier
Toltec
Sublette
Big Horn 1.4%
Lava
Antonito
Romeo 0.9%
Bountiful
La Jara
Estrella 1.0%
Alamosa

Willow Creek
Chama 1.4%
Lobato
Azotea
Monero 2.0%

Gato
Juanita
Navajo 1.4%
Dulce 1.7%
Lumberton 1.4%
Amargo

9000'
8000'
7000'
6000'
5000'

Creede

Rio Grande

Rock Creek

Alamosa Jct.

Alamosa 251.7

Estrella 259.6

La Jara 266.2

Bountiful 269.7

Romeo 273.3

Antonito 280.3

Palmilla

agosa Springs

Navajo River

Rio Chama

Rio Chamita

COLORADO
NEW MEXICO

Cumbres 330.6

Coxo 332.2

Los Pinos 324.8

Osier 318.4

Toltec 310.5

Sublette 306.1

Big Horn 299.4

Lava 290.8

Rio de Los Pinos

Cresco 335.5

Lobato 340.0

Chama 344.1

Willow Creek 349.2

Azotea 354.0

Monero 363.5

Amargo 366.9

Dulce 373.3

Lumberton 369.5

Rio Chama

Volcano

Rio Grande

No Agua

RIO GRANDE STEAM FINALE

Narrow gauge railroad photography in Colorado and New Mexico

From the collections of the
Center for Railroad Photography & Art

EDITED BY

Scott Lothes
Elrond Lawrence

ESSAYS AND PHOTOGRAPHS BY

Don L. Hofsommer
Karl Zimmermann

FEATURING PHOTOGRAPHS FROM
THE 1950s AND 1960s BY

Tom Gildersleeve
John Gruber
Victor Hand
Jim Shaughnessy
Fred Springer
Richard Steinheimer

With a gallery of recent images
by additional photographers

CONTENTS

FIRST PAGE: Detail views of K-36 and K-37 narrow-gauge locomotives by Victor Hand (upper row) and Richard Steinheimer (lower row).

PREVIOUS SPREAD: At Antonito, Colorado, where the standard-gauge rails end and only narrow-gauge track remains, Richard Steinheimer photographed a freight train steaming west into the San Juan Mountains on February 6, 1961.

OPPOSITE: K-36 engine 480 charges east near Monero, New Mexico, with a passenger excursion train making an all-day run from Durango to Alamosa, Colorado, on June 16, 1961. Victor Hand made this photograph from parallel U.S. Highway 64 in a car driven by his good friend, Don Phillips.

FOREWORD

Scott Lothes

President and
executive director

Center for Railroad
Photography & Art

THEY CAME FROM New York and New Jersey, from Wisconsin and Iowa, from Texas and California. From the far corners of the nation and many places in between, they came to the remote and rugged country along the Colorado–New Mexico border. They came to see, to ride, and especially to photograph the narrow-gauge trains of the Denver & Rio Grande Western Railroad's San Juan Extension.

In the rich annals of the railroad history of the United States, perhaps no other lines have received attention in such great disproportion to their size than the narrow-gauge railways of southwestern Colorado. From their constructions to their operations and even to their impacts on their local communities, their every aspect has been documented in enough books and articles to fill a library. What could another publication about the narrow gauge possibly offer?

For all of us at the Center for Railroad Photography & Art, the initial concept for this book was simple. As our archives have grown to approach a million images from nearly 100 photographers, artists, and collectors, we have begun to seek projects that allow us to draw from as many of them as possible. Running through most of our largest photography

collections like common threads set thirty-six inches apart are the Rio Grande narrow-gauge lines in the 1950s and 1960s.

But it's not just the presence of this material in so many of our collections that garnered our attention. Each of these photographers who covered the narrow gauge in its final years of Rio Grande operation created exquisite and powerful images—not just of one particular railroad, but of an entire way of railroading, one that defined the nation for nearly a century. The photographs in these pages are wholly and completely of their time and place, while at the same time fully transcending both.

Fate often determines when and where eras come to their ends. By 1950, the Rio Grande wanted out of the narrow-gauge business. Then an oil and gas boom in Farmington, New Mexico, demanded the rail transport of pipe and drilling supplies by the trainload, and the narrow gauge was the only way to get there. But the new business was finite: enough to keep the trains running, but not enough for new investments. While the D&RGW—like every other railroad in the nation—modernized and dieselized the rest of its lines, it made no such efforts on the narrow gauge.

This precise combination of circumstances preserved steam-era freight railroading in the

rocky San Juans until the late summer of 1968, more than a decade longer than steam lasted in most other parts of the country. For the generation of rail photographers who had grown up with steam and deeply lamented its passing, the narrow gauge was one more last chance. They came to it with better cameras and film, and with more fully matured styles and techniques, than they had available for the end of steam on their hometown railroads.

And they came knowing very well that it would soon end. More than half a century later, that sense of urgency is plainly and poignantly visible in their photographs. They went to great lengths just to visit the narrow gauge, and once there, they photographed it tirelessly and fearlessly. Every train might be the last—the last they would ever see on the narrow gauge, and the last steam freight train they might see, ever.

They found far more than the locomotives that called to them. They found railroading practices and traditions that spanned generations. They found railroaders fighting both nature and their employer to keep their trains running. They found communities built by and that still clung to the steel rails. They found the awesome and harsh beauty of a slice of the West just barely in the grasp of the modern world. Up there in the high country of the San Juans, along those narrow tracks so near to the sky, they found the very depths of longing.

As night descends over the San Juan high country at the end of October 23, 1962, a westward train climbs toward Cumbres Pass. Photograph by John Gruber

THERE IS NO CURE

Early exposures to the narrow gauge

Essay and photographs by

Don L. Hofsommer

My parents in 1952 orchestrated a two-week vacation to Colorado that included an overnight stop at Durango with intent to ride Denver & Rio Grande Western's narrow-gauge line to Silverton the next day. To our everlasting dismay, we learned that the line was out of service, but after dinner Dad and I determined to poke about D&RGW's yard and then strolled into the engine facility to admire the several silent locomotives resting there.

In a few minutes we were met by V.J. Hedrick, hostler and engine watchman, who welcomed us and seemed mildly bemused by the appearance of Iowa hayshakers disposed to ask all nature of questions about the narrow gauge and his own railroad experience. With little to do, Hedrick was amenable, regaling us with riveting tales of the rails including his personal involvement in filming the dramatic head-on collision staged above Durango along the Animas River in July 1951 as part of Paramount's *Denver & Rio Grande* movie.

Eventually I built up the courage to ask if Hedrick could offer an operating timetable, and after a lengthy search he came up with one from the 1920s, apologizing for not being able to locate a current issue. My dismay at not receiving an up-to-date version must have been apparent (shame on me), and Hedrick disappeared for a moment, returning with a D&RGW lantern, which he handed to me as a consolation. No more frowns. The Colorado narrow gauge virus: there is no known antidote, no cure, for anyone fully exposed. And I was fully exposed.

It was back to Colorado two years later—this time with Dad and John Knudsen, lifelong friend and fellow railroad enthusiast—to be part of a wondrous three-day excursion from Alamosa to Durango, Silverton, and return. We were entirely ignorant of "photo shoot" protocols, but after being recipients of a few angry shouts from the more sophisticated among us, we obediently fell into line. Well, not completely—a bit of our rebellious instincts remained.

At Durango, John and I changed out of our "railroad garb" and donned white duck trousers and blue suede shoes, which were much in fashion at the time. But apparently not in Durango, for our appearance in these duds resulted in more than a few curious stares from the locals. (Durango in 1954 was a much different place than today.)

We were then off to Silverton to absorb the beauty that had been deprived us in 1952. As it developed, D&RGW determined to add internal combustion tractive effort to our K-28 road locomotive—this to the utter dismay of all true believers. Among these was Rogers E.M. Whitaker—a.k.a. E.M. Frimbo, "World's Greatest Railroad Buff"—who for this day was fully ensconced in a cupola seat on the caboose at the head of the train. Frimbo notwithstanding, the great treat for me was meeting and spending time with another young chap, Stan Rhine, an eventual disciple of Robert Richardson and who one day might be labeled "dean" of D&RGW narrow-gauge history and operation.

On the final day of this marvelous expedition, at Chama, while our locomotive was being serviced and a helper engine lined up, somebody—I suspect James J. Kreuzberger— approached a small crowd of curious onlookers and inquired if any of them would, for a fee, drive him and a few others up to Cumbres— this for the purpose of getting photos of the train beating up the grade. As it turned out, he found a willing young man with a rickety pick-up truck. After he had solicited a dollar from perhaps a dozen other daredevils, the truck roared off in dust, its passengers bouncing unmercifully in the truckbed along unpaved Highway 17. On command the driver pulled over and occupants jumped out to make a series of photographs as the double-headed excursion train vigorously assaulted the unforgiving heavy grade. What a sight! In each instance we jumped back into that unlikely taxi, and ultimately the driver got us back to the train at Cumbres—not one of us worse for the wear, amazingly.

Ah, it was over all too soon. The Colorado narrow-gauge fever? No known cure.

RIGHT: Locomotives 488 and 492 lead a train west out of Alamosa in the summer of 1964.

OPPOSITE: Later on the same day, the train swings through curves while climbing the grade near Sublette. The tank cars are going to Chama for crude oil.

Ten years later, I was teaching at Fairfield, Iowa, and about to be married at the end of the school year in June. A tradition among many Iowa teachers at the time was to head for Colorado in the summer in order to work on graduate degrees, typically at Colorado State College in Greeley. That presented an interesting possibility. How about a summer-long Colorado honeymoon and graduate courses for both Sandy and me? *Voilà!* But what location?

Greeley is short of the mountains and long on conventional railroading. Schools in the interior? Western State at Gunnison is in beautiful country, but by then was devoid of rail activity. What about Adams State College at *Alamosa*, in the heart of the San Luis Valley and, might I add, heart of D&RGW's remaining narrow-gauge empire? End of discussion.

Adams State professors proved to be competent and demanding (especially on the Age of Jefferson and Jackson), but with classes scheduled in the mornings there was ample time in the afternoons and evenings for reading and writing. And if a steam whistle sounded late in the morning, there was time to see what those melodious tones might imply.

Business on the narrow gauge in the summer of 1964 was still fairly brisk with one or two trains each week in each direction. Pipe and drilling mud went west to the Farmington oil fields; coming east was oil from the loading racks at Chama for the refinery at Alamosa, dimension lumber from mills in Durango and Chama, and company coal from mines at Monero. Empties and a modicum of mixed freight moved in both directions.

ABOVE RIGHT: Engines 487 and 498 pull a westward train near Ignacio, Colorado, bound for Durango on June 21, 1965.

BELOW RIGHT: "Cartoads" work to maintain the ancient fleet of narrow-gauge freight cars on the open-air repair-in-place (RIP) tracks in Alamosa in 1964.

After spending most of a 1964 summer day climbing westward, 498 and 493 have reached the top at Cumbres, elevation 10,015 feet, where the sun has returned after a rain shower.

Depending on immediate needs to complete course requirements, it might be possible to follow train movements from the Alamosa yard to Antonito, perhaps to the Sublette area (take your books—it will be a couple hours before you hear the approach of the train and then see it), or maybe all the way to Cumbres. Other days could be spent watching turns from Chama wrestling tonnage up the four-percent grade to Cumbres—always a treat.

Of course there were many days at Alamosa when there was no operating activity on the narrow gauge, but on every working day there was some type of activity at the roundhouse, where boilermakers, pipe fitters, machinists, and others rebuilt or otherwise attended to the needs of D&RGW's fleet of ancient if curiously resilient narrow-gauge

steam locomotives. One could wander in and about the roundhouse uncontested, staying at an appropriate distance from whatever work was being performed. Another attraction was the RIP track, where "cartoads" labored to patch and repair D&RGW's equally ancient narrow-gauge car inventory. Roundhouse staff seemed mildly tolerant of the comings and goings of outsiders, but cartoads were surprised and pleased that anybody might be attracted by their work.

I took particular pleasure in exploring the Alamosa engine facility late at night (very late at night), especially after a train and helper from Chama had long since tied up and the two locomotives snored lightly outside the roundhouse, awaiting attention by the day crew that would appear in a few hours. The roundhouse on these nocturnal visits was eerily silent but strangely inviting, the engine watchman unconcerned by my admiration for the undersized steel monsters in his care.

My wife Sandra on occasion would take a break from her own studies and go with me to my favorite lookout near Sublette (bring your books, Sandy) or maybe even on to Cumbres or Chama. On one very dreary day we followed an eastbound turn out of Chama over a rain-soaked and very slippery Highway 17 when a couple of frightened and confused bears tumbled down onto the road and nearly into the lead locomotive before turning at great haste in front of us and scampering off to a safer haven.

Later, at Cumbres after the helper engine had turned and lumbered off to Chama, the crew on the road engine invited us into the cab. "Did you see those bears?" the engineer asked. "We certainly did," was our reply. Each of us regaled the others with our impressions of that zoological hilarity. "Want to ride down to the highway crossing with us?" the engineer asked me, the implication being that Sandy could drive the car and pick me up. Oh, my, yes, sure! But Sandy had no experience driving on roadways such as New Mexico's strangely slick Highway 17. "Uh, er, no, I'd better not," was my dismal but utterly appropriate reply. So off went the road engine, sans Don. And as it developed, no other enginemen on the D&RGW narrow gauge ever had the good taste to make a similar offer.

An increasingly favorite haunt for me was the Alamosa RIP track, where carmen always welcomed my presence, graciously responded to my questions, and showed a willingness to share memories of their work and times. Rudy Romero was the foreman, and at some point I told him that Sandy and I were new to Mexican cuisine and I asked for his recommendation as to a local eating establishment. He mumbled something in response and was noncommittal—totally out of character. I was puzzled but tried again some days later. Same response.

On the third try, however, he relented, grudgingly it seemed, and pointed off to the northwest, away from railroad property, to an absolutely nondescript building, saying that "Cy's is the best." Then he jabbed a finger into my chest, earnestly demanding that we "never go there on Saturday nights," fellow carmen nodding in agreement. I agreed, but chose not to ask why, finding out from other sources that nasty fights were not unusual in that area on Saturday evenings. Cy's? Oh yes, Rudy got it right and Sandy and I frequented the place for lunch—luxuriating in Cy's Special, a large boat of green and red chili separated by refried beans with a side of absolutely delicious sopapillas. Marvelous.

All too soon, it seemed, our summer session at Adams State came to an end and it was time to return to teaching duties in Iowa. Rudy Romero said I should stop by the RIP track on our way out of town, that he had something to send with us. He did: a well-traveled, properly stenciled RIO GRANDE stepbox, a personal treasure. The Colorado narrow-gauge virus? No known antidote.

ABOVE: The three-rail yard in Alamosa on a bright summer day in 1964.

OPPOSITE: A Cumbres Turn stomps up the grade out of Chama, approaching Lobato along "strangely slick" Highway 17 on a dreary summer day in 1964.

With the next year came rumors of an expansive private western rail tour by the R.R. Donnelley Company of Chicago that would include a special narrow-gauge train from Silverton to Durango, Chama, and Alamosa. A telephone call to the ever-efficient and helpful A.M. Ficci, D&RGW's agent and operator at Alamosa, confirmed days and times for this special, and, Ficci added, there was a significant likelihood of narrow-gauge freight movements about the same time. We plotted a Colorado adventure accordingly, and yes, a westbound freight had departed before we reached Alamosa.

A.M. Ficci, Denver & Rio Grande Western's station agent and operator in Alamosa, sits at his desk in 1964.

We headed for Sublette, one of our favorite spots where, in the summer before, Sandy and I had spent time studying, awaiting the eventual sound and then appearance of a hard-working K36/K37 pair toting a maximum of 1,600 tons toward Cumbres. (An electrical storm for the unsheltered at 9,500 feet elevation is a real adventure.) The next two days we trailed that same tonnage to Durango, encountered the Donnelley special from Silverton, and then admired it to Chama and Alamosa. Apparently there was more than a

bit of amusement/bemusement among those on the special as to that guy and gal following the train, appearing here and there to take photographs or simply to soak in the beauty of the countryside and the charm that the narrow gauge added to it.

At the Chama stop I struck up a conversation with one of the train's riders, a man I no longer can identify, who told me that the equipment would double back to Durango on the morrow as a Colorado and New Mexico Game and Parks Special, that there would be room for Sandy and me, and suggested that at least we could ride as far as Chama. How would we get back to our car at Alamosa? He would work on that, and we agreed to meet the next morning at Alamosa. There he was, as planned, saying that the Durango-based engine crew had deadheaded on the train to Alamosa instead of tying up at Chama, that they would be happy to drive our car to Chama, and that we would be welcome guests on the train. Does a bear like honey? Is the Pope Catholic? Aboard we went. Not far out of Alamosa, D&RGW's trainmaster detected that we did not look like Fish & Games personnel and inquired as to our presence. Our friendly sponsor explained that the Durango enginemen were driving our auto to Chama, where they would be ready to work through to their home terminal, and that this explained why two itinerants from Iowa were on the cars. The trainmaster was not amused. But for us it was a marvelous and totally unanticipated pleasure. The narrow-gauge virus: no known cure, no salvation.

ABOVE LEFT: Freight cars await the attention of repairmen at Alamosa's open-air RIP tracks on a summer day in 1964.

BELOW LEFT: Two of those carmen go about their tasks beneath one of the freight cars.

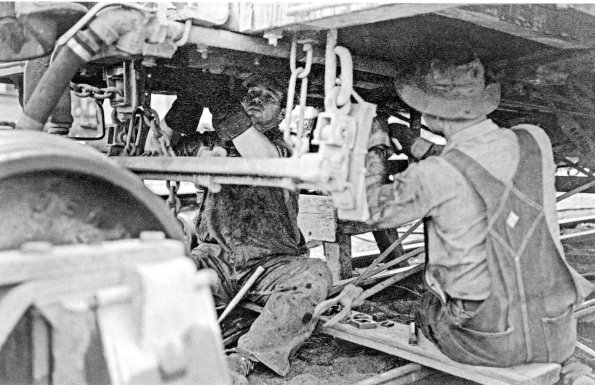

ABOVE: The little-remarked car-men in Alamosa held the rolling stock together with innovation, sweat, and know-how.

ABOVE RIGHT: Rudy Romero, foreman of the Alamosa car repairers, uses a stencil to apply lettering to a freight car.

OPPOSITE: A Cumbres Turn climbs the grade near Cresco under heavy smoke in 1964.

Another trip to Colorado in 1967 went for naught—nothing moving. A slow walk through the Alamosa roundhouse to again admire the now very silent but still valiant narrow-gauge warriors had its reward, of course, and a stroll beyond to the RIP track found the always smiling Rudy Romero and his friendly fellows laboring at their tasks of patching and servicing the dwindling car fleet. And it was a pleasure to visit with Mr. Ficci at his office. Yes, it was a pleasure … if bittersweet.

The end came soon thereafter for the narrow gauge as I knew it—the third rail removed from Alamosa to Antonito, the line abandoned from Chama to Durango and on to Farmington. But, I am very happy to say, powerful ghosts of a wondrous past live on even today in the form of the Cumbres & Toltec and Durango & Silverton—tonic, yes, oh yes, elixir, balm for those afflicted by the narrow-gauge virus. There is no cure.

ALAMOSA

Fresh off a trip to Chama and back, engine 493 rests in the Alamosa roundhouse next to engine 484 on the evening of August 29, 1967, in this photograph by John Gruber.

THE BEATING HEART of the narrow gauge in its later years was not at its geographical center but at its eastern extremity: Alamosa, Colorado. Sitting in the wide San Luis Valley at 7,545 feet above sea level, Alamosa was the connection to the Denver & Rio Grande Western's standard-gauge system and the rest of the railroad world. Workers in the roundhouse, backshop, and yard maintained the fleet of ancient rolling stock; a refinery processed crude oil that arrived in tank cars from a pipeline in Chama, New Mexico; and overhead cranes transferred freight between standard- and narrow-gauge cars—most of it bound for the oil and gas fields of Farmington, New Mexico.

Steel rails arrived in Alamosa in 1876 with the completion of a narrow-gauge route from the east over La Veta Pass. The railroad then was the Denver & Rio Grande ("Western" was added in a 1921 reorganization), under the leadership of General William Jackson Palmer. He had grand plans to reach south to Texas and Mexico while also tapping the resource-rich San Juan Mountains to the west.

The D&RG never reached the former, but it achieved the latter in 1881 with its narrow-gauge San Juan Extension to Durango, Colorado.

The D&RG converted the line over La Veta Pass to standard gauge in 1899, which led to the unusual addition of a third rail in 1901 for standard-gauge as well as narrow-gauge operation between Alamosa and Antonito. That came with the unrealized hope of extending the standard gauge south and west from Antonito, but it still proved useful. Narrow-gauge trains could run in and out of the terminal facilities in Alamosa, while the many customers in the San Luis Valley could utilize standard-gauge cars. Special idler cars even allowed the same train to carry cars of both gauges between Alamosa and Antonito.

On what remained of the narrow-gauge network by the late 1950s, Alamosa was also the closest point to Denver and Colorado's more populous eastern third. Thus it was where many visiting photographers began their explorations of the narrow gauge.

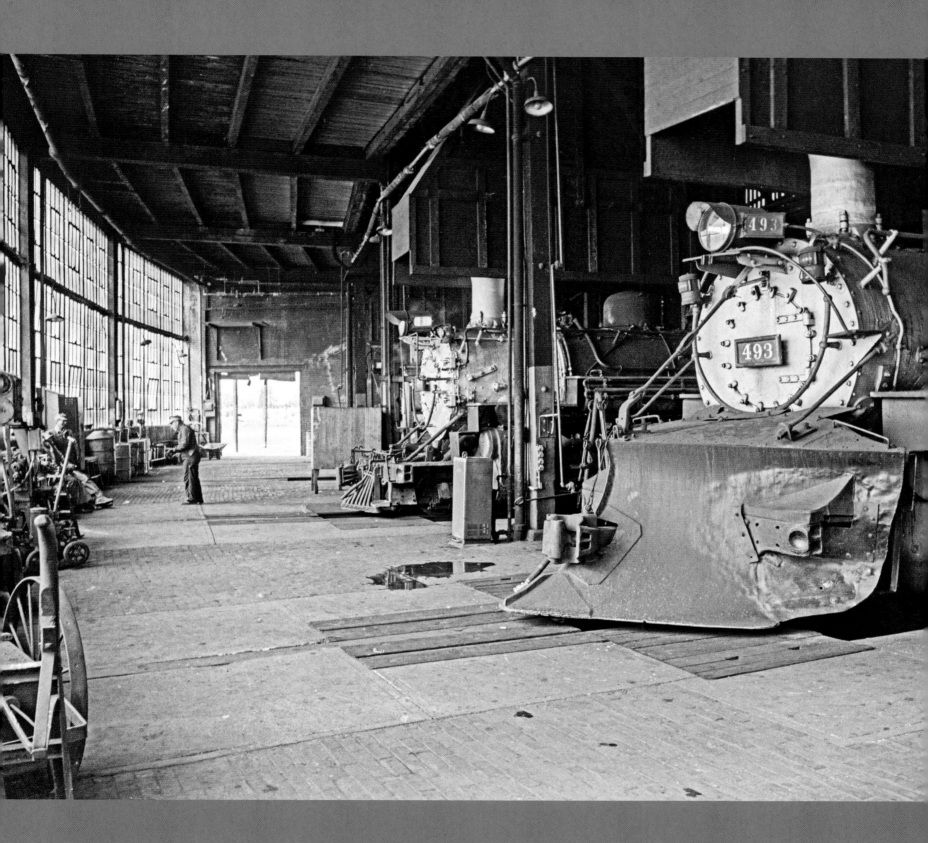

LEFT: The Rio Grande shops and workers in Alamosa maintained all of the narrow-gauge locomotives and rolling stock during their final years of operation. Richard Steinheimer photographed the chalkboard showing each engine's status during his winter visit in 1961.

PREVIOUS SPREAD: Jim Shaughnessy photographed the shops in August 1963. At left is the back shop, where heavy repair work and overhauls were performed, with K-37 class locomotive 492 as well as a smaller K-28 class engine behind it. At right, a shop worker touches up the number of K-36 class engine 487.

RIGHT: On a clear September day in 1959, Shaughnessy stood inside the roundhouse and framed a view looking out at 487 on the turntable, being readied along with 499 to take a train west to Chama.

FOLLOWING SPREAD: A little later that morning, Shaughnessy photographed 487 sitting in the yard across from the water tank, with the 14,000-foot Sangre de Cristo Mountains in the distance.

The yard in Alamosa featured transloading facilities between standard- and narrow-gauge freight cars, which Richard Steinheimer portrayed in September 1959.

ABOVE: Engineer Johnny Lira performs the time-honored tradition of "oiling round" his locomotive, the 498, as photographed by John Gruber on the morning of August 28, 1967. Along with 493 and engineer Bob Morgan, they would take a train to Chama that day. It was the next-to-last year for the narrow-gauge freight operations. After 1964, the Rio Grande had stopped keeping Cumbres Pass open in heavy snow, and trains ran only from late spring through early winter, with diminishing frequency each year. Twelve days had passed since the last train had departed Alamosa.

RIGHT: In 1961, when Richard Steinheimer made this evocative view of 483 and 481 being readied to take a train west, operations were a little brisker. The railroad was still open year-round, there was more pipeline business for Farmington, and oil still moved by rail out of Chama. That was enough for at least one or two trains each way every week. A few years earlier, though, during the peak of the pipeline boom, trains steamed out of Alamosa once or even twice a day—as quickly as freight could be transferred between standard- and narrow-gauge cars.

WEST TO CHAMA

With morning approaching midday on August 28, 1967, John Gruber photographed a westward train leaving Alamosa's three-rail yard. The Sangre de Cristo Mountains stand in the hazy distance; ahead lie the San Juans.

THE 92.4-MILE RUN from Alamosa to Chama often took twelve hours or more due to slow speeds and frequent stops for water and other maintenance, and it came in three parts. The first twenty-nine miles to Antonito were straight, flat, and relatively fast. Then came fifty miles of almost unrelenting climb to Cumbres Pass, elevation 10,015 feet, on a ruling grade of 1.42 percent with twenty-degree curves, requiring two locomotives for nearly all westward trains. The last 13.5 miles were down a four-percent grade—often after dark—that required constant vigilance to prevent runaways.

For photographers, the westward trip also came in three phases. U.S. Highway 285 and State Highway 17 (a contiguous road bearing the same number in both Colorado and New Mexico) made the first and third segments relatively accessible, but most of those fifty miles in the middle were hard to reach.

In the latter years of narrow-gauge freight operations, trains typically ran in three-day cycles, with crews called simultaneously out of Durango and Alamosa, usually around midmorning. On the first day, each of them worked from their respective terminals to Chama. The late 1950s and early 1960s often saw two train cycles per week year-round, but the Rio Grande had already begun diverting some of the narrow-gauge business to its trucking subsidiary. After a fire closed the Oriental Refinery in Alamosa in September 1964, the Rio Grande stopped keeping the line open through the winter over Cumbres Pass, and train frequency diminished during the rest of the year—averaging just one freight cycle every week . . . or two . . . or longer. The pattern remained the same, though, so a train leaving Alamosa for the west still meant three consecutive days of operations.

SOUTH OF ALAMOSA, U.S. Highway 285 closely parallels the railroad for nearly all of the twenty-nine miles to Antonito. The run is almost perfectly straight, with just two gentle curves, and nearly as flat. When narrow-gauge locomotives ran here, it was their best chance to stretch their legs—perhaps at a blistering thirty miles per hour. Between that 'speed' and the proximity of the highway, it was a prime location for pacing photographs, a staple for almost anyone who pointed a camera at the narrow gauge in the 1950s and 1960s.

While the concept was the same—drive alongside the train at the same speed and use a slow shutter speed to render the locomotives sharp and the foreground blurred—each of these four photographers came up with their own unique take.

UPPER LEFT: Jim Shaughnessy presents a classic view in August 1957 with K-36 engines 487 and 483 hustling a train of pipe and empty tank cars west.

LOWER LEFT: Taken exactly a decade later, John Gruber displays his knack for "perfect imperfection" in a back-lit view with lens flare and a pole in front of lead engine 498. Yet they add dynamism to the scene, especially with Gruber's impeccable timing that captured both engineer Lira and fireman Smith going about their respective tasks in perfect silhouette.

UPPER RIGHT: Victor Hand provided a dramatic nocturnal version of this scene by firing a no. 22 flashbulb from the backseat of his pacing vehicle, driven by Don Phillips, on the night of June 16, 1961. A third participant, Bill Westcott, rode in the trunk with a second no. 22 bulb connected by wire to Victor's camera.

LOWER RIGHT: Richard Steinheimer puts the viewer in the driver's seat right next to him in his daring, over-the-steering-wheel view from February 6, 1961.

THE CREW OF EXTRA 498 and 493 West tends to a "hot box"—an overheated journal bearing—during a stop at La Jara, Colorado, on August 28, 1967. Such delays were common on the narrow gauge, especially in its later years, as both young and veteran railroaders nursed equipment that was nearly a half-century old.

The end of revenue freight service and Rio Grande operation of the narrow gauge was barely a year away, and by this late date the trains almost always attracted a crowd; three other railfans stand in sunlight behind the two railroaders.

Photographer John Gruber was riding this train on assignment for TRAINS magazine at the behest of David P. Morgan, its legendary editor. Seeking a new take on such a well-known subject, Morgan and Gruber came up with the idea of providing a look at the narrow gauge from the perspective of the men who made it run. With a strong background in photojournalism and a deep love for the narrow gauge, Gruber was perfect for the job. He rode to Chama and back with this Alamosa-based crew, exposing nearly 1,000 frames of 35mm black-and-white film in his two Nikons. This book includes more than sixty of his photographs from that trip and four of his prior visits, many of them in print for the first time.

LEFT: While the train crew addressed the hot box in La Jara on August 28, 1967, the engine crews of 498 and 493 topped off their tenders with water from the tank, which John Gruber also photographed during the lengthy stop. La Jara is just 14.5 relatively straight and flat miles from Alamosa, and the engines wouldn't have needed water so soon, but they wouldn't reach another source until Lava, more than twenty-five miles farther and well into the climb into the San Juan Mountains. In between those points, the tank at Antonito had frozen and burst a few winters earlier, and the railroad had decided not to repair it.

RIGHT: When the Antonito water tank was still working properly, Richard Steinheimer photographed engines 483 and 481 standing on either side of it on February 6, 1961. After taking water and coal in Antonito for the long climb ahead, the crews of westbound trains would move one of the locomotives into the middle of the train since the bridge over Cascade Creek could not bear the weight of two engines coupled together.

Steinheimer's square-format Bronica camera lacked a lens wide enough to take in this full scene with both locomotives, so he took separate shots of each one. Decades later, his wife, Shirley Burman, scanned the two negatives and combined them into the single digital photograph presented here.

LEFT: On a September day in 1959, Jim Shaughnessy photographed locomotive 499 at the switch in Antonito where the narrow gauge split. Until 1942, the "Chili Line" on the left had continued south to Santa Fe, New Mexico. The line diverging to the right is the San Juan Extension to Chama, Durango, and beyond. The third rail for standard gauge operation continued just a little over half a mile farther, ending just past the U.S. Highway 285 grade crossing. The depot, which still stands and now belongs to the Town of Antonito, is visible in the distance between the two lines.

ABOVE: John Gruber caught this train departing Antonito for the west on October 23, 1962, passing a sawmill at the U.S. 285 crossing on the western edge of town. Today the Cumbres & Toltec Scenic Railroad's facilities in Antonito occupy this location.

FOLLOWING SPREAD: Where the standard gauge ended and only three-foot rails remained, Richard Steinheimer made a photograph for all time of 483 and 481 marching west into the San Juan Mountains with a train of loaded pipe cars and empty tank cars on February 6, 1961.

PREVIOUS SPREAD: West of Antonito, the railroad climbs more than 2,100 feet in fifty miles to 10,015-foot Cumbres Pass, with a ruling grade of 1.42 percent. The long, sustained climb is a workout for the locomotives and their crews, especially the firemen. Gruber made a series of pictures of Gayle Cunningham throwing coal into the firebox and resting when he had the chance. Meanwhile, Bob Morgan worked the throttle as the tank at Lava came into view through his window.

Cunningham would heave several tons of coal on the ninety-two-mile run from Alamosa to Chama, but it wasn't as bad as he had feared when he hired out as an eighteen-year-old in 1957. He had been raised on a farm near La Jara, and he told Gruber:

"I grew up shoveling grain all the time. A scoop shovel was nothing to me. On the train, there was a stopping place. On the farm, if you can't find anything to do, you fix fence. That's probably why it wasn't hard even right off. I knew how to use a scoop shovel. . . . So I liked it right off. Pretty much knew how to do the work."

ABOVE LEFT: Lava is the next water stop, eleven miles beyond Antonito on the sloping western edge of the San Luis Valley. On May 27, 1961, Fred Springer was aboard a special passenger train for the Rocky Mountain Railroad Club that performed a photo runby there. From the far side of the sweeping curve, he captured the train in profile against the broad valley and a big Colorado sky.

ABOVE: Six years later, the westward freight train that John Gruber was riding stopped at Lava for water. A pump filled the tank from the Rio de los Pinos, 520 feet below.

From the cab of 493, John Gruber looked back on the westward train of August 28, 1967, with 498 hard at work in the middle on a ledge high above Cañon Jarosito. A few minutes later, the train arrived at Sublette, where it stopped for more water and further repairs to the hotbox the crew had discovered earlier in the day at La Jara. The building is the former section house, which once housed the crew that maintained this section of the line.

LEFT: Victor Hand captured 480 blasting out of Rock Tunnel high above the Toltec Gorge in a photo runby staged during an excursion from Alamosa to Durango on June 7, 1960. Photo runbys provided rare opportunities to photograph this remote part of the line.

ABOVE: Fred Springer photographed the Rocky Mountain Railroad Club's special train of May 27, 1961, crossing Cascade Creek in a photo runby during its trip from Alamosa to Durango. The Rio de los Pinos flows in the valley at right, 175 feet below the railroad.

THE WESTWARD TRAIN OF October 17, 1967, negotiates the horseshoe curves at Los Pinos (seen here) and, several minutes later, Cumbres (following spread)—also known as Tanglefoot Curve—as the shadows grow long. The two big curves allowed the railroad to gain 400 feet of elevation without exceeding its 1.42-percent ruling grade by wrapping eight miles of track into two and a half miles of distance.

Photographer Victor Hand had followed this train with his friend Gordon Roth out of Alamosa in the morning, leapfrogging it in the remote stretch between Antonito and Los Pinos. Arriving here in the mid-afternoon, they could only wait and hope that the train would reach them before sunset. Many westward trains did not, even in the long days of summer, but the crews of 487 and 497 must have had a particularly good run with their forty-two-car train on this perfect fall day—to Hand's and Roth's delight then, and to our visual benefit now, more than half a century later.

ARRIVING AT CUMBRES late in the day on August 28, 1967, the train John Gruber was riding stopped to prepare for its descent down the four-percent grade to Chama. After climbing nearly 2,500 feet in seventy-nine miles since leaving Alamosa that morning, the train would give up nearly all of that elevation—2,152 feet of it—in less than fourteen miles and a little over an hour.

First, the crew cut out the 498 from its helper position in the middle of the train. It briefly rejoined 493 at the front for the final pull over the summit, and then it ran light down the grade to Chama ahead of the train, which would follow several minutes behind it.

FOLLOWING SPREAD: While waiting for 498 to get ahead, the brakemen turned up the air brake retainer on each car, a mandatory step to help hold back the train on the steep downhill run—and a step still taken today on Cumbres & Toltec Scenic Railroad trains. During the descent, brakeman Stanley Smith watches for overheating brakes and any other sign of trouble from his cupola seat in the train's first caboose. The railroad had added a second caboose behind it for Gruber in his assignment for *TRAINS* magazine.

LEFT: John Gruber watched and photographed the train's descent on August 28, 1967, from the seat across the cupola from brakeman Stanley Smith. Just west of Cresco, light smoke from the brake shoes wafts back through the twenty-eight cars as the train eases down the four-percent grade. Light smoke meant the brakes were working properly; heavy smoke would indicate trouble.

ABOVE: Arriving in Chama at dusk, the crew quickly tied down their train and put away their engine for the night. Chama was a busy railroad town on the night following the first day of any freight cycle, with trains arriving from both Alamosa and Durango. Their crews and locomotives would all spend the night before departing the next morning.

CHAMA TO DURANGO

The low winter sun shines through thin, high clouds to cast the shadow of 499 and its exhaust onto the snow-covered ground west of Chama in this February 1961 photograph by Richard Steinheimer.

ON THE SECOND DAY of a freight cycle, the crews that met in Chama the previous evening began their respective trips back to Alamosa and Durango, each taking the train that the other crew had delivered the day before. So the westward train that had come out of Alamosa with an Alamosa-based crew continued from Chama to Durango with the crew that had come from Durango the day before.

The 107.4-mile run from Chama to Durango wasn't quite as dramatic as the trip over Cumbres Pass, but it still made for an interesting day of railroading or photography. Ten up-and-down miles west of Chama, the line crossed the Continental Divide in an unremarkable cut at an elevation of 7,733 feet and then descended for more than forty miles down the Navajo and San Juan Rivers to 6,100 feet on grades as steep as two percent. In 1962, the Army Corps of Engineers realigned the railroad around Arboles, New Mexico, because of the construction of the Navajo Dam, adding nearly four miles to the length of the line—and the most modern track on the system. The route then climbed over two summits: a small one at Tiffany and a larger one at Falfa, both with a ruling grade of 1.42 percent that usually required a second locomotive. From Falfa, the route descended to the Animas River at Carbon Junction on seven miles of two-percent grade and then had a short climb over the last two miles into Durango.

Three miles west of Chama, Richard Steinheimer photographed a trio of horses watching 499 leading a train to Durango on February 3, 1961. The railroad left Chama at a southwesterly angle, then turned west, swinging around Rabbit Peak to run along the southern escarpment of the San Juan Mountains, seen in the background. Real horses still run here along the base of the San Juans, but iron horses haven't passed since a clean-up train ran west on December 6, 1968.

LEFT: The westward train of October 7, 1965, climbs out of Willow Creek, New Mexico, five miles west of Chama, behind 483 in this color photograph by Victor Hand. Five miles west of Willow Creek, the railroad crossed the Continental Divide through a nondescript cut next to U.S. Highway 84, at an elevation of 7,733 feet—nearly 2,300 feet lower than Cumbres Pass.

RIGHT: On July 14, 1961, Fred Springer caught 486 and 480 with an unusual double-headed westward train that included two flat cars of special equipment ahead of a typical consist of pipe and boxcars. He photographed the train four miles west of Willow Creek (above) and again, five miles farther on (below), at the U.S. Highway 84 crossing; in the distance is Briggs Mesa, standing more than 1,100 feet above the road and track here at an elevation of 8,602 feet. The railroad skirts its base to the left and enters a canyon carved by Amargo Creek and containing the coal mining community of Monero, which was established by Italian immigrants in the 1880s.

LEFT: The last revenue freight train on the narrow gauge between Chama and Durango steams west over the Florida River in this Victor Hand photograph from August 29, 1968. Read more about this day on page 72.

RIGHT: Richard Steinheimer used a dramatic September sky in 1959 to render caboose 0540 in silhouette at the rear of a westward freight train near Ignacio, Colorado.

FOLLOWING SPREAD: Another pairing of Hand and Steinheimer photographs portrays helper operations on this stretch of the line. At left, Hand's photograph shows 494 with its train stopped at the west siding switch of Gato next to 480, which had come from Durango to assist this train west on June 14, 1961.

Two years earlier and farther to the west, Steinheimer made this poetic view of 487 and 483 pulling a train of boxcars and pipe along the San Juan River under a cloud-dappled late-summer sky just east of Arboles. While the grade was downhill here, the line would soon climb out of the San Juan's drainage on a 1.42-percent ruling grade to Tiffany. This stretch of track was relocated in 1962 due to the Navajo Dam, adding nearly four miles. After a short descent, there was a much longer climb of nearly twenty-three miles, also with a 1.42-percent ruling grade. After reaching the summit at Falfa, the helper engine usually cut off and ran solo the remaining ten miles to Durango, with the train following behind it.

ON THE MORNING OF August 29, 1968, the last revenue freight trains departed Chama in both directions. Victor Hand and his friend Don Phillips photographed the eastward train climbing the four-percent grade at Windy Point, and they then doubled back to catch up with the westward train steaming toward Durango.

Hand desperately wanted to photograph a train climbing the grade to Falfa in the sweeping curve just south of Florida, and this was his last chance. His previous attempts had failed when the trains arrived here after sunset, but with a short consist and no need for a helper engine, 483 and her crew made good time and came stomping up the 1.42-percent grade in the midafternoon, with the two brakemen enjoying the ride atop the first boxcar. Hand quickly reloaded his Speed Graphic, turned to this right, and exposed a second sheet of 4x5 color negative film, capturing Rio Grande's narrow-gauge freight operations rolling into eternity.

More than fifty years later, trains still climb the four-percent grade from Chama to Cumbres, but the track between Chama and Durango is nothing but a memory.

DURANGO

WHILE ALAMOSA MAY HAVE been the heart of the Rio Grande narrow gauge in its later years, its soul was Durango. The railroad built the town at the beginning of the 1880s as it pushed the San Juan Extension toward its goal of Silverton and that bonanza of precious-metals mining. The initial boom ended with the Panic of 1893, but the trains steamed on and the mines rebounded before eventually playing out. A smelter operated on the western bank of the Animas River just south of the engine terminal from 1882 until 1930. It reopened during World War II to produce uranium for the Manhattan Project, closing for good in 1963 and leaving behind a complicated legacy.

For most of the first half of the twentieth century, narrow-gauge lines fanned out from Durango on four points of the compass, including the Rio Grande Southern, with its spectacular but ill-fated line to the west and north. Immortalized by Lucius Beebe and scores of other authors, Durango—with its classic depot, water tank, coaling tower, and centerpiece ten-stall roundhouse—became a place of pilgrimage for railroad lovers from across the country and even beyond. While the backshop in Alamosa handled heavy repairs, Durango's 1882 roundhouse maintained engines for freight trains to Chama and Farmington, as well as the passenger trains to Silverton. And while Farmington provided the bulk of the freight business in the 1950s and 1960s, Durango had its share—particularly from the Weidman Sawmill, a stalwart shipper until the end of narrow-gauge freight service.

ABOVE: Headquarters of railroading in Durango was and remains the two-story 1882 depot at 479 Main Avenue. Fred Springer photographed it in 1953, when it housed the Denver & Rio Grande Western; today it is home to the Durango & Silverton Narrow Gauge Railroad.

RIGHT: Fred Springer found 493 steaming past the Graden Flour Mill on May 31, 1958. The mill stood just west of the yard near the Animas River; the vehicles in the photograph are on U.S. Highway 160, which crossed the river to the left of the image. The track curving off to the left also crossed the river; it provided access to the smelter and connection with the Rio Grande Southern Railroad, which was abandoned and dismantled in the early 1950s. The Graden Mill stood until 1976; it is also visible in the left background on the next page.

ABOVE: Tom Gildersleeve's October 1962 photograph shows the Durango engine facility, with Perins Peak behind it. In the distance at right are the snow-capped La Plata Mountains, which rise to 13,000 feet. This scene changed greatly in the late 1960s with the construction of a new highway interchange here between U.S. 160 and 550.

ABOVE RIGHT: Following a trip to Hermosa, brakeman Myron Henry uses his brake club on the handbrake of a work train in front of the Savoy Hotel in Tom Gildersleeve's photograph from March 19, 1963.

FOLLOWING SPREAD: John Gruber and Richard Steinheimer share some of the mystery of the night that enveloped the railroad in Durango. Gruber aimed his Nikon into the roundhouse in August 1967, recording examples of the three classes of locomotives that predominated on the narrow gauge in its latter decades: K-28 478, K-36 487, and K-37 498. Six years earlier, Steinheimer's long exposure captured a trail of light left by a worker inspecting 487 on the evening of February 1, 1961.

DURANGO ENGINE WATCHMAN Ed Kettle poses inside the roundhouse next to the ancient coal stove on the evening of January 30, 1961, and tends to 487 two nights later. Richard Steinheimer made these photographs for his landmark book *Backwoods Railroads of the West* (Kalmbach, 1964). Kettle was first startled and then perplexed when Steinheimer showed up at the roundhouse with his first wife, Nona. Stein's handwritten note on the envelope for his negative tells the story:

"We surprised him late at night, as he was shoveling coal and wishing for spring. He couldn't believe Nona and I had come <u>there</u> from California."

Durango could be a magical place, especially on clear and cold winter mornings when an engine was working in the yard. The crisp light and big clouds of steam offered endless photographic possibilities, and no one was better at taking advantage of them than Richard Steinheimer. On February 1, 1961, he found 483 next to the coaling tower, rendering its striking form in silhouette. Two mornings prior, he made a portrait of 473 with its distinctive diamond stack—an aesthetic modification to the K-28 locomotives for the Silverton tourist trade—wreathed in its own exhaust.

The morning of February 1, 1961, found Rio Grande railroaders in Durango preparing engines 494 and 483 to take a train east to Chama, as portrayed by Richard Steinheimer. Visible at far left is 464, the only member of the K-27 class that remained by this time. Built in 1903, it would be retired the following year.

LEFT: A yard crew with locomotive 478 switches boxcars in the upper end of Durango's yard in this Richard Steinheimer photograph from January 30, 1961. Halfway back, a brakeman stands on the roof of a car to relay hand signals between the engineer and the brakeman riding the end. While the steam locomotives were the biggest draw for photographers of the narrow gauge, these other aspects of traditional railroading were ultimately just as endangered as the engines and added much visual interest.

ABOVE: Two and a half years later, on August 26, 1963, John Gruber made this photograph of three locomotives in the Durango yard. In the middle background is 464, which had become a parts source for other locomotives by this time but would ultimately be preserved, residing in Michigan in 2023. Steamed up at left is much larger K-37 498, which would lead a train east to Chama that day.

FARMINGTON TURN

A Farmington Turn steams down the Animas River and away from Carbon Junction in this Richard Steinheimer photograph from January 30, 1961. In the foreground is the main line heading to Chama and Alamosa.

AN OIL AND GAS BOOM in Farmington, New Mexico, that began in 1951 was the reason narrow-gauge freight operations lasted as long as they did. After taking two days to go to Chama and back, the Durango-based crew made a round-trip to Farmington and back on the third day, which concluded that particular freight cycle. Compared to the rest of the narrow-gauge, the 47.7-mile Farmington Branch was a leisurely stroll.

Westward trains carrying mostly pipe and drilling supplies rolled down the Animas River on grades of one percent and curves no sharper than seven degrees. The return trip up the river consisted of mostly empty cars—easy work for a single locomotive and its crew. Other than Farmington, the only water source was in Bondad, Colorado, and it was rarely used since the quality was poor, and most trains could make it all the way back to Durango after filling up in Farmington.

Yet the branch had its charm—from the vistas of the broad river valley, to its many wooden trestles and one major bridge, to the switching and servicing operations at either end of the run. The branch also had an unusual history, having been built as an isolated standard-gauge line in 1905—as a deterrent to possible incursions by the Santa Fe or Southern Pacific from the south and also for the unrealized hopes of someday converting the entire San Juan Extension to standard gauge. The Rio Grande gave up that dream in 1923 and relaid the Farmington Branch to narrow gauge, a rare example of a gauge change from standard to narrow in all of railroad history. The last trains ran in 1968, and the tracks were completely gone before the end of 1971.

ABOVE: Two miles south of Durango, the crew of a Farmington Turn with engine 494 "drops" their caboose into Carbon Junction on October 19, 1960. Trains coming west from Chama typically set out the cars that were destined for Farmington at Carbon Junction; the next day, the Farmington Turn would pick them up and take them to Farmington. Because of the downward-sloping grade, a dropped caboose would roll into position, which made putting the train together at Carbon Junction more efficient. Photographer Tom Gildersleeve watched with amazement as the caboose coasted for a great distance.

RIGHT: In March of 1963, another Farmington Turn crosses the Animas River just south of Bondad. The train has recently exited New Mexico on its way back to Durango. Tom Gildersleeve also took this color photograph.

FOLLOWING SPREAD: The Farmington Branch's wooden trestles could make for interesting photographs. Tom Gildersleeve made the color view of 492 leading a train back to Durango near Carbon Junction in March 1963. Two years earlier, Victor Hand used two no. 22 flashbulbs to illuminate 491 returning to Durango after dark on June 15, 1961.

A long Farmington Turn led by engine 487 rolls down the wide valley of the Animas River north of Bondad in this Victor Hand photograph taken from the side of U.S. Highway 550 on October 13, 1965. In the distance at right are the La Plata Mountains, twenty-five miles to the northwest. The Farmington Branch followed the Animas River for the entirety of its forty-seven miles. Compared to most other stretches of the narrow gauge, this line was a cakewalk, with curves no sharper than seven degrees and a ruling grade of one percent. It was a rare example of a line that had been built as standard gauge and converted to narrow gauge.

RIGHT: The fireman of engine 491 poses at Farmington on January 30, 1961, for Richard Steinheimer. Below him hangs a common detail of Rio Grande steam locomotives: the canvas water bag, whose clever design cooled water by evaporation.

OPPOSITE: Earlier that day, Steinheimer photographed 491 approaching a short bridge east of Bondad, where snow that had fallen since the last run to Farmington still covered the rails.

VICTOR HAND, ALONG WITH Gordon Roth, photographed 498 steaming down the Animas River with pipe for Farmington as it passed the water tank at Bondad on October 19, 1967. U.S. Highway 550 followed the tracks but was on the other side of the river here; reaching this location required a walk across a pedestrian suspension bridge made of rope and wood, where Hand, Roth, and Roth's wife, Gail, posed for a photograph with three of their four cameras.

Six years earlier, when he was still in high school, Hand had driven to the narrow gauge from his home in New York. He posed with friends on the pilot of 491 at Farmington for a self-portrait on June 15, 1961, standing second from right. His lifelong friend Don Phillips is second from left, directly under the engine's number plate. Hand and Phillips would make another trip to the narrow gauge together in 1968 to catch the last revenue freight trains. That time they flew to Denver and rented a car. They punched a hole in its oil pan on the rough road west of Lava, but quickly had it repaired and enjoyed a fine day of photography on August 29, 1968—see page 72 for more about that.

AFTER RIDING THE train from Alamosa to Chama and back on August 28 and 29, 1967, John Gruber (with his wife, Bonnie, and son, Richard) drove to Durango and chased the next day's Farmington Turn.

PREVIOUS SPREAD: John's many fine photographs from that day include this incredible pacing shot of 498 steaming across one of the line's many wooden trestles, taken from the passenger seat of his Rambler American while Bonnie drove.

CLOCKWISE FROM RIGHT: At the end of the branch, Gruber made a series of pictures of the engine and train crew members going about their tasks. Engineer Gibbs and fireman Tafoya pose in the cab window and gangway; Gibbs oils the 498; Tafoya fills the tender; a trainman uses his brake club to tie down the hand-brake on a freight car; and the same trainman drops off the caboose, club in hand, as another member of the crew watches from the cupola.

DURANGO TO CHAMA

DURANGO WAS THE WESTERN starting point for narrow-gauge freight cycles, typically dispatching a train for the east on the same day Alamosa sent a train west. After following the Animas River south for 2.4 miles to Carbon Junction, the line climbed away from the river on 7.5 miles of two-percent grade to Falfa. Trains heavy with lumber from the Weidman Sawmill or even long trains of empty pipe and drilling supply cars required a second engine to make that grade. Most of the eastern half of the run to Chama was uphill, too, again sometimes requiring a helper engine.

While photographers frequently prioritized the more spectacular portion of the line to the east between Chama and Antonito, those who followed trains between Durango and Chama found many rewards. They also documented a segment of the railroad that no longer exists. The last trains ran in 1968, and the tracks were removed in 1970 and 1971.

Engines 497 and 491 pull past a string of stock cars at Durango on October 20, 1962. After passing the switch, the locomotives would back up, couple to their train, and head up the grade to Falfa. Tom Gildersleeve's photograph shows the smelter across the Animas River in its final year of operation.

LEFT: Storming east out of Durango, 487 and 489 add their exhaust to the heavy sky near the top of the 7.5-mile climb up the two-percent ruling grade from Carbon Junction to Falfa. Jim Shaughnessy recorded this scene in September 1959.

PREVIOUS LEFT: A little earlier on the same morning, Shaughnessy caught the same train approaching Carbon Junction, two miles out of Durango along the Animas River. 487 would assist road engine 489 to the top of the grade at Falfa.

PREVIOUS RIGHT: 483 and 494 lead another train east up the same grade a year and a half later, passing an automobile graveyard on February 2, 1961, in a classic scene of the West by Richard Steinheimer.

FOLLOWING LEFT: Under stormy skies on August 26, 1963, John Gruber photographed 498 leading a train east over weed-grown track in Oxford, Colorado, nineteen miles out of Durango. Stock cars sag in the siding at left, likely staged for loading in the fall.

FOLLOWING RIGHT: Later on the same day, a brakeman walks boxcar roofs with his wooden brake club—used for leverage when tying down brake wheels. Gruber used the tall cumulus clouds and strong vertical lines to create an iconic photograph of this since-vanished scene that had once been part of every freight train.

MIDDAY SUNLIGHT SPARKLES on the San Juan River, which engine 473 has just crossed with a special passenger train from Durango to Alamosa on October 3, 1965, trailing a long plume of smoke in this spectacular Victor Hand photograph. Just ahead of the train lies the confluence of the San Juan and Navajo Rivers. The train will follow the latter for nine miles to the station at Navajo, where the tracks head up the canyon of tributary Amargo Creek.

What is now the U.S. Southwest is the traditional homeland of several Native American tribes. Today the Navajo Nation encompasses parts of northwestern New Mexico and northeastern Arizona, as well as a little of southeastern Utah. The Rio Grande narrow gauge reached a corner of it at Farmington, New Mexico. Between Durango and Chama, the tracks also passed through the Southern Ute and Jicarilla Apache reservations.

Three miles in the other direction from this spot is Gato, previously called Pagosa Junction, where a branch line extended thirty-one miles north to Pagosa Springs—a hub of logging operations— until its abandonment in 1935. Another five miles west of Gato was the siding at Carracas, the regular meeting point for the *San Juan* passenger trains— numbers 115 and 116 (changed to 215 and 216 in their final years)—every afternoon until their last runs on January 31, 1951. After that date, the only passenger trains between Durango and Alamosa were special excursions, which the Rio Grande operated with some frequency into the mid-1960s for railroad clubs and other groups.

CHAMA

IN ITS RAILROAD HEYDAY, Chama boasted a nine-stall roundhouse with activity around the clock, serving as a base for helper engines and snow-fighting efforts on Cumbres Pass. Only echoes of that past remained in the final years of freight operations. Much like the mining towns that had lured the railroad in the nineteenth century, Chama was a place of boom or bust on the narrow gauge in the late 1950s and 1960s.

With trains and their crews starting from Alamosa and Durango, Chama was quiet until the first evening of a freight cycle, when those two trains arrived. The next morning brought a flurry of action as both train crews, usually working with three engines, prepared for departure. Eastward trains often required two or even three trips to get all their cars up the four-percent grade to Cumbres, but once that was accomplished, the quiet returned. Chama's yard and engine terminal then sat silently, perhaps stirred briefly by maintenance workers, awaiting the next call for freight service.

On the evening of the first day of each freight cycle, the two trains—one from Durango and one from Alamosa—would meet in Chama and spend the night there. Victor Hand skillfully combined six no. 22 flashbulbs with ambient lighting to illuminate two of the locomotives at rest long after sunset on October 11, 1965. Chama had once boasted a nine-stall roundhouse, but seven of them were torn down in 1946. With only two stalls remaining, most engines stayed outdoors. While the crews usually turned back to their home terminals from Chama, the locomotives often continued in their direction of travel. The 487 had come in from Alamosa and would lead the train to Durango in the morning, while the 483 had come from Durango and would lead two Cumbres turns the next day.

ABOVE: The call board in Chama listed the trains, start times, engines, and crew assignments for the next day's operations. When John Gruber arrived on the evening of August 28, 1967, it showed two trains: an EE (Extra East) at 9a (9:00 A.M.) with 497 and 493, engineers Lira and R. Morgan, and firemen S. Smith and Cunningham; and an Extra West at 8:15 A.M. with 498, engineer Gibbs and fireman Tafoya. The white "Notice" posted at the top of the board is about an exhibition of railroad photographs by Frank Barry, many of which appear in his outstanding book, *The Last Winter*.

OPPOSITE: Four years earlier on August 27, 1963, Gruber stood inside the engine house and looked out at 488 next to the coaling tower, preparing to depart on its second trip to Cumbres that day.

FOLLOWING SPREAD: From his room in the Hotel Shamrock, Richard Steinheimer photographed two girls walking under its sign in 1961. Across Terrace Avenue are the Rio Grande yard and shops.

On the last day of revenue freight service, August 29, 1968, Victor Hand looked through the depot's bay window and made this photograph showing a worker's hands writing at the operator's desk.

Ranchers and railroaders prepare to load sheep into livestock cars for shipment by narrow-gauge train. Victor Hand made these two photographs at the Chama stock pens on October 8, 1965, during the next-to-last season for livestock shipments on the railroad.

RIGHT: On the morning of October 3, 1967, Victor Hand climbed the coaling tower in Chama to record this view looking north (east by the railroad's timetable) with 493 and 498 in front of the water tank. They had brought the train from Alamosa the day before, and both of them would continue to Durango on this day, while 497 and 487 would make two Cumbres turns.

OPPOSITE: Heavy clouds hang over Chama on a September morning in 1959 as railroaders and locomotives prepare for another day of operations. Jim Shaughnessy positioned himself low between 483 and 499, providing a sense of scale and wonder prior to their run up the four-percent grade to Cumbres Pass.

Frank Morrow was a master mechanic who helped keep the narrow-gauge trains running through the end of Rio Grande operations. Based in Alamosa, he drove a company pickup truck to meet the trains in Chama every time they ran in their final years. John Gruber photographed him chatting with the Durango-based engine crew of the 498 and posing on their train's caboose, 0540, on the morning of August 29, 1967.

ABOVE: Ice covers much of Chama's water tank as engines 480 and 483 prepare for a somewhat unusual day on March 14, 1963. They will take eight loaded tank cars, a flanger-spreader, and two cabooses to Cumbres, leave the tank cars there, and continue with the rest to Alamosa. Photographer Tom Gildersleeve managed to follow them a few miles up the pass before snow-covered Highway 17 became impassable for his car, even equipped with chains. After a 170-mile detour over Wolf Creek Pass, he caught the train again between Antonito and Alamosa (see page 171).

ABOVE: Engine 480 fills the crisp morning air with big clouds of steam on October 21, 1962. It will soon head west with a train to Durango, while 483, along with 497, will make two turns to Cumbres. Photographer Tom Gildersleeve opted for the latter; see pages 137, 156, and 157 for more of his results that day. Also note that two young children can be seen enjoying a cab ride in 483.

FOLLOWING SPREAD: Cumulus clouds drift above the yard as 498 and 488 stand ready for their second trip to Cumbres in this John Gruber photograph from August 27, 1963. Their train was eleven tank cars of crude oil from the Gramps pipeline in town, bound for the Oriental Refinery in Alamosa.

CUMBRES TURN

Engine 487 with its massive snowplow sits in front of the Cumbres depot—which had formerly been the section house—in a strong juxtaposition by Richard Steinheimer in September 1959.

ARGUABLY THE MOST spectacular stage on the Rio Grande narrow gauge was the four-percent grade from Chama to Cumbres. Engines worked hard and the scenic highlights were plentiful, including 100-foot-high Lobato Trestle, S curves on the mountainsides around Cresco, and ruggedly spectacular Windy Point just before reaching the 10,015-foot summit of Cumbres Pass.

In the last years of freight operations, two engine crews and two locomotives often had to make two or even three trips to get all the cars in one train up the grade. On the day after bringing a train west from Alamosa, the same crew members would make a "Cumbres Turn" from Chama to Cumbres and back. After lunch, they would head up the grade again with more cars. If a third trip was required, they would return to Chama, spend another night there, and go back up the grade the next morning. Once they had all the cars at Cumbres, the crew would put their train back together and depart for Alamosa.

With slow train speeds and Highway 17—albeit not yet paved—closely following the tracks all the way, a photographer could catch each train several times in those 13.5 miles. The road crossed the railroad three times and offered a different vantage point around every turn. The light and even the weather could change dramatically from morning to afternoon, offering endless variety on days when two trains went up the grade. This was the show that photographers from across the country came to see, and it was where they produced some of their most stunning work.

LEFT: Just north of Chama, the track crosses the Rio Chama on two through trusses and passes the distinctive "Jukes Tree," made famous by photographer and Rio Grande railroader Fred Jukes in the first decade of the twentieth century. On October 12, 1965, Victor Hand recorded 483 leading a Cumbres Turn past the tree, with a bulldozer on a flat car coupled to the tender. Freight trains often carried equipment to clear rock slides and do other work in the railroad's many difficult-to-reach places.

ABOVE: Three miles northeast of the Jukes Tree, the railroad crosses Wolf Creek on 100-foot-tall Lobato Trestle, where Tom Gildersleeve photographed the second Cumbres Turn of October 21, 1962. Engines 483 and 497 were hefting eleven loaded tank cars—maximum tonnage for the two locomotives—up the four-percent grade to 10,015-foot Cumbres Pass.

LEFT: The lead engine of a Cumbres Turn throws a massive cloud of smoke and steam into a leaden sky at the spot where the railroad diverges from the road just below Lobato. Jim Shaughnessy made this view in September of 1959.

ABOVE: On August 27, 1963, John Gruber followed two trains up the pass. This was the first one, crossing Lobato Trestle in the morning, with the 498 and 488 moving one tank car of crude oil, five flat cars of lumber, and seventeen boxcars.

OPPOSITE: Horses run between Jim Shaughnessy's car on rain-slickened Highway 17 and the railroad, where engine 483 leads a train of empty pipe cars from Chama to Cumbres on a cold September day in 1959.

LEFT: Engine 499 drifts down the grade near Cresco in an early snowfall in September 1959. It had helped 483 on a freight train coming west from Alamosa that day, but Jim Shaughnessy's photograph conveys the essence of the many light-engine movements down the grade following uphill trips from Chama to Cumbres.

On two October days six years apart, John Gruber and Victor Hand photographed Cumbres Turns snaking through two different sets of S curves near Cresco. At right is Gruber's late-afternoon view from October 3, 1961, with the 494 pulling an eighteen-car train of oil loads and pipe empties, assisted by 486. On the facing page, Victor Hand presents the 487 leading a train to Alamosa from a location known as Hamilton's Point with the unseen 483 pushing on October 10, 1967, a day when low traffic allowed the two engines to take all their cars up the hill in a single trip.

LEFT: Snow can come early to the high country, and Tom Gildersleeve found a winter wonderland on October 18, 1960. He also found 483 and 491 on a Cumbres Turn of empty pipe cars approaching the west switch at Cresco under vortices of smoke and steam. Nearly every photographer to visit the narrow gauge has depicted a train from this superb roadside vantage point, but perhaps none any better than Gildersleeve did here, the only time he ever made it to Cumbres Pass in snow.

ABOVE: Gildersleeve soon overtook the train and caught it again, this time approaching the road crossing near Coxo, below Windy Point.

STATE HIGHWAY 17 IN BOTH New Mexico and Colorado, unpaved until the late 1960s, follows the railroad between Chama and Los Pinos. Its crossings were and remain popular locations for photographers chasing trains up the four-percent grade. On October 3, 1961—his first serious day of photographing the narrow gauge (he had visited previously on vacations with his parents)—John Gruber stopped at the crossing between Dalton and Cresco. There he captured a late-afternoon Cumbres Turn in silhouette against the still-lit mountainside across the Wolf Creek Valley. Parked by the track is a 1929 Graham Paige sedan, which two other rail enthusiasts, Andrew Wittenborn and Frank Barry, were driving across the country.

Six years later, on August 29, 1967, during his last trip to the narrow gauge in the Rio Grande era, Gruber was at the crossing near Coxo using two cameras to make a sequence of photographs as 493 and 497 stormed up the grade with a train for Alamosa. This was part of Gruber's assignment for *TRAINS*, which published a series of four telephoto images of this scene. The magazine did not use the wide-angle view shown here, which takes in the breadth of the valley as the two smoke plumes mingle with storm clouds already building in the late-morning sky.

FOLLOWING SPREAD: Three photographs by Fred Springer from the stormy afternoon of July 14, 1961, show an action sequence at Coxo. 491 whistles for the crossing, 497 thunders behind it, and the whole thirty-two-car train wraps around Windy Point a few minutes later, a mile and a half farther and 300 feet higher.

From the lofty height of Windy Point, John Gruber looked down into the Wolf Creek Valley on August 27, 1963, and captured seemingly all of the grandeur of the narrow gauge in a single photograph. Shadows grow long as the afternoon sun lowers in the west while 498 and 488 approach the road crossing just below Coxo with the day's second trip to Cumbres: eleven cars of Gramps oil from the pipeline in Chama, bound for the refinery in Alamosa.

STANDING NEAR TRACK LEVEL at Windy Point on two different days in the fall of 1967, Victor Hand portrayed the drama of freight trains climbing the four-percent grade to Cumbres.

LEFT: On October 18, he photographed 487 and 493 on a train heavy with lumber. No Cumbres Turns operated in this freight cycle; this was the only eastward movement, and after the 493 cut out from its helper position at the summit, both it and the 487 with the train continued to Alamosa (pages 160-161).

RIGHT: Two weeks earlier, on October 3, 497 and 487 hammered up the grade under a dramatic sky. Business was sufficient for two Cumbres Turns on this day, with a third trip the following day, after which the reassembled train proceeded to Alamosa.

FOLLOWING SPREAD: Two photographers present two views of the snowshed covering the tail of the wye at Cumbres. At left, Hand photographed the 484 exiting the shed after turning on October 7, 1965. Two years earlier, on August 22, 1963, Jim Shaughnessy stood inside the shed to frame the same engine, this time in helper service with the train's caboose.

On October 21, 1962, Tom Gildersleeve photographed two Cumbres Turns bringing eastbound cars up the grade from Chama to Cumbres. 483 led each run, with 497 helping. After both trips, each locomotive turned on the wye at Cumbres and returned to Chama. These two photographs show the 483 in the same spot—between the standpipe and the depot (formerly the section house)—after each run.

On the previous page, Gildersleeve stood at the
west siding switch and framed the scene with the
depot and snowshed covering the wye. On this
page, a few hours later, with twilight draining from
the sky, he captured the 483 and the stand pipe
in silhouette as night descends on the high country
and another day of narrow-gauge freight railroading.

RETURN TO ALAMOSA

AFTER THE CLIMAX OF the climb to Cumbres, the rest of the trip back to Alamosa was the denouement—almost all downhill, literally as well as figuratively. The run lacked the excitement and drama of many other parts of the narrow-gauge operations and could even carry the melancholy notion of conclusion as another freight-train cycle came to an end. In the last few years, it could be many days or even weeks before the next trains ran.

Yet for the train crews, the trip back to Alamosa meant a return to their homes and families. Their eastward trains were sometimes tasked with supporting maintenance work along the line, offering chances for different kinds of photographs for those inclined to seek them. Operating patterns occasionally led to meets between narrow- and standard-gauge trains on the dual-gauge track between Antonito and Alamosa. That long, flat, straight stretch along U.S. Highway 285 still afforded opportunities for pacing shots, too. If the timing was just right, the setting sun might provide a final flourish on a narrow-gauge train returning home.

On March 22, 1963, engines 483 and 480 bring a flanger-spreader set of snowfighting equipment into the Alamosa yard beneath a colorful sky. Photographer Tom Gildersleeve said the train took thirty-six hours to make it to Alamosa from Durango, during which it derailed and was rerailed several times.

Engine 487 and caboose 0574 bracket the twenty-three-car eastward train of October 18, 1967, in Victor Hand's diptych at Tanglefoot Curve, immediately east of Cumbres.

A section crew dumps ballast to shore up a soft spot in the roadbed at Los Pinos in these three John Gruber photographs from August 29, 1967. In the final years of its narrow gauge operations, the Rio Grande rarely ran dedicated work trains, instead using regular freight trains for these tasks. The train Gruber was riding had picked up these three cars of scoria at Cumbres, and the section crew used their motor car to meet the train here.

While all of the Rio Grande train crew members were white at this time, these and many other maintenance workers were of Hispanic ancestry. In 2014, Gruber reconnected with Gayle Cunningham, who was firing engine 493 on this day. Gruber interviewed him for an article in TRAINS magazine, and Cunningham said:

"My best friend, Frank Archulete, was Spanish from La Jara, and when I hired out I told him the railroad was a pretty good place to work. I didn't want to tell him but finally had to tell him: they wouldn't hire him [for train service]. The only place they would was on the section gang. That was hard to tell, but he understood."

LEFT: The section crew pushes their motor car back onto the main line from its set-out track at Los Pinos as the eastward train departs on August 29, 1967. Photographer John Gruber rode in one of the train's two cabooses from Cumbres all the way back to Alamosa.

ABOVE: Gruber used one of the train's rear marker lights to frame this view of engine 493 steaming past the railroad's facilities at Osier, twelve miles east of Cumbres, which included a water tank and section house.

ABOVE: With storm clouds boiling over the San Juans, 497 approaches Antonito late in the afternoon of August 29, 1967. The engine had helped 493 get its train up the grade to Cumbres that morning, and then ran light—by itself—all the way back to Alamosa, standard practice on the railroad at the time. Bonnie Gruber made this lyrical photograph of a little engine in a big land as she and her young son, Richard, waited here for her husband, John, who was riding the following train.

RIGHT: Narrow- and standard-gauge locomotives meet on the three-rail trackage at Antonito on August 22, 1963. Jim Shaughnessy spent the day following a narrow-gauge train east from Chama all the way to Alamosa. Helper engine 484, running ahead of the train with road engine 488, had to wait at Antonito for the arrival of a standard-gauge local freight train from Alamosa behind GP7 diesel-electric locomotive 5104.

FOLLOWING PAGE: Later that afternoon, Shaughnessy photographed 488 leading the narrow-gauge train past the depot in La Jara.

PREVIOUS PAGE: The eastward train of August 29, 1967, stopped briefly in La Jara, where the crew inspected some of the lumber it was carrying. John Gruber photographed conductor Delmer Smith watching with his grandson, who lived in town and came out to meet his grandfather's train.

LEFT: Evening sun illuminates 480 rolling off the final miles of its all-day run from Durango to Alamosa with a passenger excursion on June 16, 1961. The shadow of Victor Hand's chase vehicle on U.S. Highway 285, driven by Don Phillips, appears at lower left.

ABOVE: The colorful sunset of March 14, 1963, silhouettes 483 and 480 as they steam toward Alamosa with a flanger-spreader snow-clearing train. Tom Gildersleeve had photographed them at Chama that morning, where they also took eight cars of oil up to Cumbres, and then he made a very long drive to avoid snowbound Highway 17 and catch the train again at day's end.

ABOVE: Engine 488 leads a short and somewhat curious train to Alamosa along U.S. Highway 285 in this Jim Shaughnessy photograph from August 22, 1963. Ahead of eight cars of oil are three cars of pipe, with four empty flat cars for spacing. Nearly all pipe shipments on the narrow gauge went west; these may have been rejected by the buyer or could have been destined for reuse elsewhere.

OPPOSITE: Shaughnessy photographed the same train arriving in Alamosa later that day after it picked up eleven stock cars. The two-story brick depot at right was completed in 1909, replacing a wooden structure from 1893 that had burned in 1907. Listed on the National Register of Historic Places in 1993, the depot houses the Colorado Welcome Center of Alamosa as of 2023.

Arriving back in Alamosa at the end of their all-day run from Chama on August 29, 1967, John Gruber photographed the crew of Extra 493 East quickly tying down their train, removing the marker lights from the caboose, and taking their locomotive to the roundhouse. It would be thirteen days before the next narrow-gauge freight train would depart Alamosa for the west.

Brakeman Stanley Smith and conductor Delmer Smith walk along the three-rail yard in Alamosa, carrying their grips from their caboose back to the depot where they would "mark off" to end their workday. Directly beyond them are two Rio Grande semi trucks parked in front of the depot. In 1959, with traffic from the pipeline boom waning, the railroad had successfully petitioned the Interstate Commerce Commission to use its trucking subsidiary as an alternative to the narrow-gauge trains, gradually diverting more business from steel wheels to rubber tires as a run-up to the end of narrow-gauge freight operations in 1968.

While several more narrow-gauge trains would run before the end of 1967, only nine revenue freights—five west and four east—ran in all of 1968, with the last ones operating exactly one year later (see page 72). John Gruber and his family would conclude their 1967 visit by traveling to the opposite end of the narrow-gauge system to photograph the next day's Farmington Turn as well as the Silverton passenger operation before driving home to Wisconsin. When they returned years later, only part of the railroad remained—and it had changed greatly.

THE SILVERTON

IN CONTRAST TO THE sporadic, waning freight-train operations, passenger traffic to Silverton was both predictable and growing in the 1950s and 1960s. After the silver and gold booms went bust, rail service to Silverton fell into a laid-back rhythm of mixed-train service (carrying both freight and passengers) making a round trip from Durango. Frequency fell from daily-except-Sunday in 1932 to just once a week during the winter of 1949. Patronage that year amounted to some 2,000 riders—an average of fewer than forty per trip and hardly enough to fill a single coach. But then Hollywood and the nation's burgeoning, vacationing, postwar middle class discovered the charms of a steam-powered ride up the remote and rugged Animas Canyon to the Victorian-era storefronts on Greene Street, and everything changed.

In 1953, *The Silverton* ran triweekly and carried 12,000 passengers. That had nearly tripled to 35,000 by 1960 with daily summer service. New equipment soon allowed for a second train on busy days, and ridership grew to 65,000 by the mid-1960s. When the Interstate Commerce Commission approved the Rio Grande's abandonment of the rest of the San Juan Extension, it called the 45.6-mile Silverton Branch too popular to let go. The railroad grudgingly embraced it, helping launch Durango's transformation into a tourist destination and luring Alexis McKinney, assistant publisher of the *Denver Post*, to run the operation.

Yet photographers as well as train crews generally preferred the freights on the rest of the narrow gauge. For photographers they were both rarer and more dramatic, while railroaders enjoyed their slower pace and lack of scrutiny. Days on the freight trains might be long, but Silverton jobs worked seven days a week with far more public interaction. Still, railroaders and fans alike could appreciate *The Silverton* for both the trains and the jobs it provided as the freights became less and less frequent.

LEFT: Passengers prepare for departure from Durango, elevation 6,522 feet, on August 25, 1963, and later enjoy the open-air car on the rear of their train in the Animas River Canyon in these John Gruber photographs. By this year, annual ridership was approaching 50,000—four times what it had been just a decade earlier, and enough for two trains to Silverton and back on this day.

RIGHT: Engines 478 and 473 prepare to take water from the Needleton tank with a special train for the Rocky Mountain Railroad Club on May 29, 1960, which Fred Springer rode and photographed. The elevation of the railroad here is 8,277 feet; snow-covered Mountain View Crest in the background stands at nearly 13,000 feet. There was once a town here, with a post office that operated from 1882 until 1919; a flood in 1927 destroyed the depot. Needleton is still a flag stop for the Durango & Silverton Narrow Gauge Railroad, mainly used by hikers and backpackers.

LEFT: The Rocky Mountain Railroad Club train of May 29, 1960, performs a photo runby at Elk Park behind engines 473 and 478, as photographed by Fred Springer—along with dozens of other riders. Most of them would have been pleased by the straight smokestack of lead engine 473, lending the K-28 a more original appearance. As *The Silverton* grew in popularity with tourists as well as Hollywood, the Rio Grande installed diamond smokestacks (like the one seen on trailing engine 478) on its three remaining K-28s— much to the chagrin of most rail enthusiasts. The Rio Grande utilized the width of the valley at Elk Park to build a siding as well as a wye for turning locomotives and snowplows. It remains a popular spot for photo runbys, and also as a flag stop for hikers and backpackers.

ABOVE RIGHT: A mile downstream and a few hours later on the same day, Fred Springer photographed the Rocky Mountain Railroad Club train about to cross the through-truss bridge over the Animas River at Elk Park on its way back to Durango. After the bridge was damaged by a flood in 1964, the railroad built a new bridge just to the east and left the old bridge standing.

BELOW RIGHT: The fireman of engine 473— which is once again sporting a diamond stack—peers out from the cab window at Silverton in this John Gruber photograph from August 25, 1963.

LEFT: As his train rolled into Silverton, elevation 9,318 feet, on August 25, 1963, John Gruber made this photograph from the last car as it passed the depot. Smoke in the distance from a work crew burning scrap wood near the railroad bridge over Mineral Creek gives the appearance of a following train—and there were, in fact, two trains to Silverton on this day. Sultan Mountain and Grand Turk, both 13,000-footers, dominate the background, with U.S. 550, the "Million Dollar Highway," winding up their northeastern flanks.

RIGHT: Upon arriving in Silverton, Gruber made a series of pictures showing the train and its passengers in town. Following its initial boom as a mining town in the late 1800s, Silverton has enjoyed a much longer boom thanks to the tourism that began to pick up in the 1950s. The railroad has been instrumental to both, hauling away the former and bringing in the latter.

A work train out of Durango steams through the Hermosa Meadows on the morning of March 19, 1963, captured in perfect silhouette by Tom Gildersleeve. While passenger business began to boom on the Silverton Branch in the 1950s, there was almost no revenue freight traffic left. Occasional work trains like this one offered nearly the only chance to see something that looked like a freight train, and they were highly coveted by visiting photographers. This train was headed by K-37 492, and the crew told Gildersleeve it was the first run of anything heavier than a K-28 on that line.

The Silverton, with engine 473, eases along a narrow, rugged ledge near Rockwood in this William E. Botkin color photograph from June 1976. Eight years after running its last freight trains over Cumbres Pass, the Denver & Rio Grande Western was still operating the narrow-gauge line between Durango and Silverton, where tourist passenger business was booming. The D&RGW continued running trains on the Silverton Branch through 1980, then sold it. With new ownership came a new name: the Durango & Silverton Narrow Gauge Railroad.

HOW I LEARNED
TO LOVE (AND LOSE)
THE NARROW GAUGE

Essay and photographs
by Karl Zimmermann

The course of relationships may be bumpy, and love is often unrequited, though occasionally there are second chances. These realities are true not just in human romances but with other passions as well, passions like mine for the Denver & Rio Grande Western's narrow-gauge railroads. It was where the amazing—both heartwarming and heartbreaking—coda of an enterprise and culture played out. And, in a happy eventuality, the story wasn't quite over when it apparently ended in 1968.

When I first saw the Rio Grande slim gauge, I liked it, but not obsessively and not entirely for the right reasons. Both my first and second visits were with Roger Cook, my friend and neighbor then and now. They would, in fact, have been impossible without him. Like me, he was a fan of steam locomotives, and from the summer of 1957 until the spring of 1960, we'd traveled all over the eastern United States and Canada in search of the dwindling few that were still in operation. Most of those engines were big; small was acceptable but not necessarily preferred.

"The narrow gauge was basically just steam that was still running," Roger confirmed as I was writing this. Fully understanding the magic of the Rio Grande's little trains—their diminutiveness, their history, their humanity, the spectacular rugged terrain they traversed, their uniqueness, the genuinely heroic nature of their survival, battling both nature and the corporation that owned them—would come later. Still, the narrow gauge was a draw for us, but farther afield than other ventures.

The complex logistics that in July 1960 brought Roger and me to Durango, the heart of the surviving narrow gauge, started in Salt Lake City, my mother's birthplace. I was there this time with both her and my father, and with his support I'd conjured a plan. We'd identified Grand Junction, Colorado, as the jumping-off place for the narrow gauge, since it was just a two-and-a-half-hour drive from there to Silverton. The *California Zephyr* served Grand Junction, and it later would carry us three Zimmermanns and Roger to Chicago. Roger would fly to Grand Junction, where I'd meet him at the airport and get a rental car.

But here's the thing. Roger had had his driver's license for nearly a year (mine was two months away) but was too young to rent a car. The solution: Dad would fly with me from Salt Lake to Grand Junction, rent a car for us, then fly back. I dearly hope I appreciated at the time his act of faith and generosity.

So on July 25, 1960, Roger and I headed south from Grand Junction through Montrose, Ridgway, and Ouray. From there we drove the magnificent if unnerving (curving, cliff-hanging, guardrail-free) "Million Dollar Highway"—so named, according to one account, because as its complex construction was contemplated in 1920, someone quipped that it would cost a million dollars to build. We traveled through the Uncompahgre Gorge and past the old mining town of Red Mountain to Silverton—like Ouray, evocative of the Victorian era.

We followed Mineral Creek into Silverton, tracing the route of the Silverton Railroad, one of "Pathfinder of the San Juans" Otto

Mears's three northerly probes. Like the other two—the Silverton Northern and the Silverton, Gladstone & Northerly—it was stymied by mountains in the quest to reach its goal of a connection to lines north.

As the road leveled off, we looked south down the Animas Canyon and saw the tower of smoke that represented our first encounter with the D&RGW narrow gauge: *The Silverton* coming up from Durango. (The train was such an institution by this time that the "T" was typically capitalized, as if it were a regular "name" train.) We knew it was scheduled into town at 12:40 P.M. and timed our arrival to photograph it as it turned on the wye before dropping its passengers. Like most of them did during their two-hour layover, we grabbed some lunch in town.

Then the train headed back down the rugged canyon into a virtual no-man's-land, its inaccessibility challenging photographers but delighting riders with stunning vistas. We waited in Rockwood, where it emerged, then followed its leisurely jog across the Hermosa Meadows to Durango. There we checked into the Strater Hotel, a Victorian classic built in 1887, for four nights. (There would be more nights for me over the decades ahead.) The next day we rode *The Silverton*—a use of time that we would retrospectively question.

Although it seemed endangered then, *The Silverton* would do nothing but thrive in the future. The train we rode was not the mixed of fond recall but in a touristic though not-yet-modernized format: two gondolas filled with ties, a baggage car and combine

with concessions, and several coaches—all original, all wooden. They were painted yellow rather than the green that had long been the Rio Grande standard, a change prompted by the train's growing movie stardom. The other even more unfortunate result of catering to Hollywood's desires was the addition of ersatz diamond stacks to the three K-28s—473, 476, and 478—that remained on the property. (Seven others had gone to the White Pass & Yukon during World War II, never to return.)

By the time we visited, 473—used as the Durango switcher and so equipped with pilot and tender footboards and a metal shield over the air pump—was straight-stacked again. The phony stacks would be removed in 1981, when Charles E. Bradshaw, a citrus magnate from Orlando, bought the branch from the Rio Grande for $2.2 million and made substantial improvements, especially to the right-of-way, allowing the use of larger locomotives than had typically operated on the branch. By 1989, his Durango & Silverton had six locomotives hauling up to four trains a day—and carrying 240,000 passengers.

The all-day journey we made aboard *The Silverton* had the exhilaration of newness, no doubt not just for the steam locomotive and magnificent scenery but also because I spent much of it at the forward-facing window of the baggage car's front door with Gervaise, a redheaded girl from Lake Charles, Louisiana, who was my chronological age but older otherwise. That fed a growing interest that for a time would push trains somewhat aside. That said, I made my best image of the trip from

Engines 481, 486, and 476 simmer inside the Durango roundhouse on a late July evening in 1960.

that window, of the fireman chaining down the spout from the yellow-wood, metal-banded water tank at Needleton to slake 476's thirst.

Back in Durango we walked to the engine terminal and found K-36 engines 481 and 486 just arriving from Chama with a few freight cars and a caboose. The balance of their train—flats with pipe, idler cars, and boxcars laden with drilling mud—had been left behind at Carbon Junction. The following morning these cars would be taken to the oil town of Farmington, New Mexico, an easy run down the Animas River Valley, wide there, behind K-37 495, and we'd be following them. In the afternoon the 495 worked back to Carbon Junction with empties, which the next day 481 and 486 would haul to Chama.

The accessibility of Durango's roundhouse and engine facilities back then was astonishing by today's standards. The freight operations at the time were in the hands of nine of the original ten K-36s (Baldwin-built in 1925) and the surviving nine K-37s from among the ten rebuilt in the railroad's Burnham Shops in 1928 and 1930 from standard-gauge 2-8-0s (Baldwin, 1902). The K-36s, with a tractive effort of 36,200 pounds, and the K-37s, just slightly higher at 37,100 pounds, were used mostly interchangeably. These locomotives mingled with the slightly older trio of K-28s and lone K-27 "mudhen" 464—though it would soon be cannibalized for parts. All four classes were 2-8-2 Mikados with outside frames. Though not much bigger than the "mudhens," the K-28s were mechanically advanced and so dubbed "sport models" by

the crews. We wandered around with our Rolleiflexes, watching the turntable point locomotives to their stalls in the roundhouse for the night, photographing the rituals of sanding, watering, coaling, and all that made operating steam locomotives—here and everywhere else—expensively rich in human activity, its charm and its downfall.

On Thursday we followed the double-headed K-36s as they ran east, climbing up the grade from the Animas River Valley to Falfa, then drifting over dry New Mexico washes, through Florida, Ignacio, Arboles, to Gato, where the engines took water. The Gomez

The fireman of *The Silverton* waters engine 476 at Needleton on July 26, 1960.

General Store, which became fan-famous with an old-style Conoco pump in front, may have been closed and didn't attract our attention. We persevered another four miles to Juanita, where the tracks crossed the San Juan River on a triple span. Here we were stymied as the gravel road petered out, so we headed back to Gato—once called Pagosa Junction, since until 1935 a branch ran north to Pagosa Springs.

We did the same as the branch had, then drove to Chama hoping that the eastbound train would catch up with us or the westbound from Alamosa would arrive off Cumbres Pass. We had dinner at Kelly's Shamrock Café, and still the Chama yard was quiet. Neither train showed before dark, so we drove back to Durango. *The Silverton* would leave at 9:15 A.M.

the next morning, but we couldn't wait. We had to make the long drive back to Grand Junction, turn in our rental car, and get to the station in time for the eastbound *Zephyr*'s departure at two minutes before noon.

My second visit came seven years and change after the first, and again Roger was the engine that powered it. He had become a true devotee of the narrow gauge during a successful 1966 trip, and a year later he chose to share this with me—and my wife, Laurel, as we'd been married the previous December. On Saturday, August 12, 1967, Roger scooped us up at the Denver airport and drove us to Chama—white-knuckled from Antonito over Highway 17. It was gravel on the east side of

Cumbres Pass, but down the west side, where grading and sometimes relocation were in progress, the road was a slough of mud and the clay binder that was a preparation for paving. We spent the night at the Elkhorn Lodge in Chama and left the next morning for Durango, where I rented a car, and Laurel and I checked into the Strater. Meanwhile, Roger, a naval officer who less than a month earlier had gone to Albuquerque to attend nuclear weapons school, drove back there.

Through Roger I knew that the typical three-day operating cycle began on Mondays with trains leaving Alamosa and Durango for Chama, continued the next day with returns to those endpoints, and concluded on the last day with a Farmington Turn. We learned that this would be delayed two days, but how bad could two days in Durango be? Laurel and I watched 473 ready *The Silverton* and putter around the engine terminal, then still with many of its 1880s appurtenances. At the Strater, we listened to the player piano at the hotel's Diamond Belle Saloon, where waitresses in throwback fishnets brought our old-fashioneds. Then we wandered just a few blocks to the roundhouse, where the doors were metaphorically thrown open to us.

"I remember that visit viscerally," Laurel reminisced. "The warmth, welcome since Colorado evenings are chilly even in August, and the soft light of the overhead bare bulbs. The hiss of steam and its smell, mixed with a tinge of hot grease. The softly panting engines. The peacefulness. The novelty of a place I'd never been before." For me, it also

might have seemed a quietude that would lead to activity the next day, which it did, as Laurel and I chased trains—and in just three days, I became truly besotted by the Rio Grande narrow gauge.

First, the 498 headed east for Chama with a train of boxcars of lumber from Durango's Weidman Sawmill—a great supporter of the narrow gauge, rejecting Rio Grande Motorway trucks when the company tried to substitute them—and empty pipe flats that had come up the branch from Farmington to Carbon Junction. Laurel and I followed the route

RIGHT: The evening sun casts long shadows as engine 493 leads a westward train down the four-percent grade into Chama on August 16, 1967.

OPPOSITE: A little later that evening at the Chama yard, four boys watch as the crew puts the train away.

Roger and I had traveled in 1960, photographing the train working hard on the grade to Falfa, taking water at Gato, and crossing the wide, channelized San Juan River just east of Juanita. The highlight of that chase came in Monero, New Mexico, with the afternoon sun dropping into the lovely light favored by photographers. Here the Mikado stopped for water, completing a perfectly arranged scene: water tank, Rio Grande standard; a trestle over a summer-dry wash; and a modest outbuilding; all against a background of sage-dotted hills.

From there the evening unfolded as if scripted: Chama was alive with steam, just as Roger and I had hoped it would be but wasn't seven years before. Laurel and I first drove toward Cumbres and caught 493 drifting down toward the Narrows with twelve boxcars of drilling mud bound for Farmington and four gondolas of scoria (volcanic cinder that the railroad used as bargain ballast). Helper engine 497 had already run down the grade light, and when 498 arrived from Durango, Chama was bustling in the evening sun.

RIGHT: The fireman of 497 prepares to fill its tender from the two-spouted water tank in Chama on the morning of August 17, 1967, in preparation for a westward run to Durango.

OPPOSITE: Late in the afternoon of the same day, clouds have rolled in as 493 takes water at Cumbres following its second trip up the four-percent grade from Chama.

When we'd photographed our fill, we crossed the street from the engine terminal for dinner. I knew I wanted to eat again at Kelly's Shamrock Café, which in spite of its Irish name specialized in Mexican food. It was Laurel's and my introduction to sopapillas, the puffy fried pastry that we slathered with honey. Then we did some night photography against a moonlit, cloud-streaked sky.

The next morning the three engines chuffed back to life. Their crews coaled them at the sooty red tower, filled sand domes, watered them at the double-spouted tank, and readied both east- and westbound trains. The 497 headed for Durango with the drilling mud and scoria, but we focused our attention on Cumbres and the two trips it would take to assemble a train there, along with twenty-one cars left there two weeks earlier. From Chama would come the boxcars of lumber from the Weidman Sawmill plus three flat cars of lumber from the local Skyline Lumber Company, and a dozen empty stock cars. These cars gave the first Cumbres Turn the look of a stock train, but the last ever of those had run the year before. No doubt my "stock train" consisted

Rio Grande Steam Finale · NARROW GAUGE RAILROAD PHOTOGRAPHY IN COLORADO AND NEW MEXICO

of cars no longer needed and destined to be scrapped—probably burned, with metal parts salvaged from the ashes. But it was photogenic.

Though frustrated by the construction we'd driven through six days earlier—I have vivid, bitter memories of being stopped by flagmen and hearing the exhaust and whistling of Cumbres-bound trains pass me by—that day was the *crème de la crème* of the narrow gauge for me, the finest time I would ever have there. Cumbres was the best: locomotives turning on the wye through the snowshed and taking water from the plug across from the section house and finally, at dusk, the 493 leaving light for Alamosa and 498 drifting downgrade around Tanglefoot Curve, its amplified train of sixty-two cars nearly filling the loop. Then we headed back to Durango for the next day's Farmington Turn.

Powered by 497, it unfolded much as it had for Roger and me in 1960—unspectacular compared to the line between Antonito and Chama, but a memorable day: the bridge at Bondad over the Animas River, trestles short and longer, and sagebrush, water stops, and the crew chatting with young boys on bicycles. It was a fine way to end our three steamy days. We had to drive to Denver the next morning to fly home, but I knew we'd be back.

So Roger had cast the metaphorical fly, I had eagerly set the hook, and the much-coveted, colorful "trout" of the narrow gauge was on my line … sort of. A wily trout, as I know well from fishing, can throw the hook or break the line as I am bringing it to net.

That's just what happened to me in August 1968, when Laurel and I returned to Colorado, totally in the thrall of the narrow gauge.

That had been our plan from the time we left Durango the August before. At home in New Jersey I bought and read books, everything I could find about the Colorado narrow gauge. *Little Engines and Big Men*, Gilbert Lathrop's first-person working account, stands out in memory. ("That's a book I'm taking to my grave," Roger says.) At a card table in the cramped kitchen of Laurel's and my studio apartment I built wooden models of D&RGW freight cars. And we planned.

We were both teachers, which meant we had summers off, but to fund jaunts like the Colorado trip we envisioned we had to teach summer school, which lasted through July. So it wasn't until August 2, 1968, that we boarded the *Broadway Limited* to Chicago, where we caught the *Denver Zephyr*. We learned that some freights had run on the narrow gauge in June and again in July, and since we were committing about three weeks to the quest, we were optimistic.

We would spend those weeks waiting for trains that never came, but we still have fond memories. We explored the narrow gauges that once were. We walked stretches of the much-lamented Rio Grande Southern, picking up a double-headed Greer spike (on my desk now); photographed Lizard Head, the rock that RGS used as a logo; found Galloping Goose 5 at Dolores, Colorado, never suspecting that I'd see it and others of the gaggle operating half a century later;

Clouds streak across the moonlit sky above Chama on the night of August 16, 1967, as 493 and 497 rest outside the enginehouse after bringing in a westward train from Alamosa. The next day, 497 would take that train to Durango, while 493 along with 498 would make two trips to Cumbres before returning to Alamosa.

drove abandoned narrow-gauge rights-of-way, including Rio Grande's Marshall Pass line and Denver, South Park & Pacific's cliff-hanging route across the Palisades to Alpine Tunnel; fished for trout on the Taylor River.

Inspired by the Strater and Sandra Dallas's *No More Than Five in a Bed*, we slept in other Victorian-era hotels in Telluride, Cripple Creek, and Central City. At this time, before skiing and casinos, they were mostly down-at-the-heel and affordable. At the Strater we usually opted for what it called "sleeping rooms" on the top floor: economical, Spartan, bathroom down the hall. But one night we sprung for a glamorous room in the corner tower with bay windows, one of which looked down West Seventh Street to the railroad.

We were lazing in that room, enjoying its elegance, when, some time after *The Silverton* had left, we heard whistling and the chuffs of locomotive exhaust. I rushed to the window and saw 473 with a box car and caboose in tow, Silverton-bound.

"Work train," I shouted to Laurel, and we were on our way. We caught up before Hermosa, where the locomotive took water, picked up a string of drop-side gondolas filled with ballast, and headed to Rockwood and then into the canyon to do trackwork. We followed it all the way to Silverton and back, a fine day of photography.

We met John and Susie LePrince, a couple from California of roughly our age who were equally hooked on the narrow gauge and like-wise waiting for a train. We explored together, haunted shops for memorabilia, and shared

meals, including grand breakfasts at Durango's Chief Diner. We went to Gato and, with no train to distract us, visited the Gomez general store: "Ruben. G. Gomez. Gen Merchandise Sheep Cattle & Wool" writ large on its modest false front. One night in Silverton we thriftily shared a motel room—not five in a bed but two, in two doubles, all on the up-and-up. Everything was memorable fun, but not what we'd come for: freights over Cumbres. The Rio Grande cited mudslides and washouts, but of course they simply didn't want to run trains.

The LePrinces stayed on, but on August 22, Laurel and I departed on a circle tour to the West Coast and back to feed another obsession—the last of the great streamliners—by riding the *California Zephyr*, *Cascade*, and *City of Portland*, leaving us in Cheyenne, Wyoming, where we'd rent a car to chase a Union Pacific excursion behind the 8444. The LePrinces would be there for the excursion, too, and by prearrangement we met at the Cheyenne roundhouse on the afternoon of August 30, the day before the trip.

They had news that devastated me then, and that I still haven't fully gotten over. While we were gallivanting around the West by rail, the cork had popped and out came the narrow-gauge freights, on August 27, 28, and 29: a trip to Gato from Durango, caboose hop back, then runs in both directions the length of the line. The final Farmington Turn came two days later.

I was stunned at the time and disconsolate for years: such a near miss and no chance ever again to make up for it, since those were the

RIGHT: The Cumbres & Toltec Scenic Railroad ran a "clean-up" train on July 17, 1971, with engine 484 running from Antonito to Chama, picking up freight cars left along the way. Near day's end, the train eases down the four-percent grade into Chama.

OPPOSITE: Earlier that afternoon, the clean-up train steams past the water tank at Los Pinos.

last revenue freights ever to ply the San Juan Extension. The wonderful pictures we made of the 8444, the rides on the streamliners that would soon be as lost as the narrow gauge would be, should have been some compensation, but they weren't. I'd loved and lost.

We had no way of knowing at the time that the states of Colorado and New Mexico would purchase the line from Antonito to Chama, sixty-four miles of railroad heaven, or that the Cumbres & Toltec Scenic Railroad would exist. When it became clear that C&TS would begin passenger excursions early in the summer of 1971, we vowed to be there, and this time the Cupid of train-infatuation shot straight and true.

When the previous winter had shut down the consolidation of all C&TS equipment in Chama, some freight cars had been dropped along the way, and on July 17, the 484 left Antonito to sweep them up. It was a freight, albeit non-revenue and caboose-less, but with boxcars, reefers, gondolas, and flat cars, it was a consist evocative of times past, and I was there to shoot it. That I did, at Lava, Los Pinos, Cumbres Pass, and on into Chama—a gift just for me.

STEAM ENCORE

WHEN THE VERY LAST train arrived in Durango from the east on December 6, 1968—a non-revenue equipment move from Alamosa—only the future of the Silverton Branch seemed hopeful. Rio Grande operations continued there, and both ridership and train frequency continued to increase. While much of the rest of the narrow gauge would be scrapped and salvaged in less than three years, a grassroots effort to preserve its most spectacular part began to grow.

In 1970, the states of Colorado and New Mexico jointly purchased the sixty-four miles between Chama and Antonito, and the Cumbres & Toltec Scenic Railroad was born. Passenger trains began running the following summer. Some of the railroad's most loyal devotees formed the not-for-profit Friends of the Cumbres & Toltec Scenic Railroad in 1988. Their volunteer and fundraising efforts help preserve and maintain the railroad, while also providing educational programs and docents. Trains run daily from late May through October, carrying some 40,000 passengers annually.

After 1980, Rio Grande finally exited the narrow-gauge business by selling the Silverton Branch to Charles E. Bradshaw, who reopened it as the Durango & Silverton Narrow Gauge Railroad the following year. A pair of sales in 1997 and 1998 brought the railroad to its current owner, Allen C. Harper's American Heritage Railways. Patronage swelled alongside Durango's rebirth as a tourist and recreation destination. Prior to the COVID-19 pandemic, annual ridership was nearly 200,000—among the highest of any tourist operation in the country.

In addition to their regular passenger trains, both railroads occasionally operate special trains for photographers, often made to look as historically accurate as possible. These are especially popular on the Cumbres & Toltec, whose equipment roster includes dozens of freight cars left over from the Rio Grande days. While these two heritage railroads have different markets and business models, both provide a remarkable continuation of the narrow-gauge story in the ruggedly beautiful San Juan country.

As the first quarter of the twenty-first century draws to a close, pairs of narrow-gauge 2-8-2 steam locomotives still power trains through the San Juan Mountains.

ABOVE LEFT: With the cottonwoods along the Rio Chama at peak fall color on October 6, 2017, Justin Franz photographed K-36s 487 and 489 leading the day's eastward passenger train past the Jukes Tree, as iconic as ever more than 100 years after its namesake first photographed trains here. Compare this scene on the Cumbres & Toltec Scenic Railroad to Victor Hand's photograph from 1965 on page 136.

BELOW LEFT: On a fall day in 2022, farther up the grade to Cumbres and with the aspens peaking under a dazzling autumn sky, Rick Malo photographed another pair of K-36s, 484 and 488, leading the train out of Chama.

RIGHT: A drone flown by Nicholas D'Amato provides a new perspective on the bridge over the Animas River just south of Silverton, where K-28s 476 and 473 lead a big fifteen-car train for the Durango & Silverton Narrow Gauge Railroad on July 18, 2022. This is the same bridge that appears in Karl Zimmermann's photograph on page 188-189.

PREVIOUS SPREAD: The first rays of February 4, 2021, have just peeked over the San Juans, casting a warm glow on the towering cliff walls above the Animas River as Durango & Silverton 476 lets off a mighty blast of steam along the High Line in this photograph by Anthony D'Amato.

BUILT IN THE NINETEENTH CENTURY and still operating in the twenty-first, the narrow gauge lines welcome visitors from near and far with an evolving and devoted mix of employees and volunteers.

ABOVE LEFT: Tourists from Japan pose with Durango & Silverton 486 at the station platform in Durango for photographs with cameras and smartphones on September 24, 2018, as witnessed by Elrond Lawrence.

BELOW LEFT: During the trip to Silverton later that morning, Lawrence caught the train crew punching tickets and trading laughs with passengers aboard the club car *Alamosa*.

RIGHT: In proud defiance of the word "brakeman" on her hat, Cumbres & Toltec railroader Elaine Zook peers back from a coach window at photographer Rick Malo during a 2022 trip.

RAILROADING IN THE SAN JUANS is still hard work, but the tracks are in far better shape than they ever were during the final decades of Rio Grande ownership, thanks to efforts of the maintenance crews on the Durango & Silverton and Cumbres & Toltec. In some instances, descendants of Rio Grande narrow-gauge railroaders continue to perform the same work their fathers and grandfathers performed.

LEFT: Durango & Silverton maintenance-of-way crews have to work with speed and precision in between trains on the tight turns and narrow ledges of the High Line. Anthony D'Amato photographed four of the workers in this crew fixing the track on November 3, 2021. Earlier that year, on June 20, while passengers were enjoying lunch in Silverton, he caught Jonathan Spiegelhalter swinging a spike maul in front of his Fairmont track speeder.

RIGHT: The Cumbres & Toltec's Chama yard was bustling with activity on the morning of October 6, 2017. Justin Franz crouched low for this view of a conductor talking to a fireman before departure as hostlers filled the sand dome of K-36 locomotive 489.

WITH ITS FLEET OF historic equipment and spectacular scenery, the Cumbres & Toltec is even more popular for photographers than its Rio Grande predecessor. The railroad frequently operates special trains chartered by groups of rail enthusiasts seeking to re-create the glory days of the narrow gauge while using the train to reach places few photographers ever ventured during the Rio Grande era. A devoted volunteer group called the Friends of the Cumbres & Toltec helps make this possible.

ABOVE LEFT: With its tender temporarily re-lettered "Rio Grande" instead of "Cumbres & Toltec," 489 steams east across Cascade Creek near Osier, Colorado, on September 30, 1981. William E. Botkin took this photograph during a charter organized by Bill Peter.

BELOW LEFT: During another photo runby at Cascade Creek on the following day, Botkin recorded most of the group of photographers.

RIGHT: Two years later, during another Bill Peter photo charter, Botkin climbed the steep mountainside to show 482 leading a train east through the spectacular rock formations at Phantom Curve near Toltec, New Mexico, on October 12, 1983. Early railroaders gave the location its name for the way their trains' headlights played off the rocks at night.

LEFT: 478 throws an enormous plume of smoke and steam into the cold winter air along the Animas River between Tacoma and Cascade on February 11, 2007, with a charter train organized by Dave Gross that photographer William E. Botkin was riding. The Durango & Silverton brought year-round operation back to the Silverton Branch, which the Rio Grande had run only during the summer and fall in the later decades of its tenure. In addition to occasional specials like this one, regular passenger trains run through the winter between Durango and Cascade, where a wye allows the entire train to turn.

FOLLOWING SPREAD: Snow still comes early to the high country of Cumbres Pass, where Nicholas D'Amato used his drone for this dramatic view of 484 leading a special train called the *Toltec Rattler* past Windy Point on October 24, 2022, at the end of the operating season for the Cumbres & Toltec.

The Cumbres & Toltec's stable includes steam rotary snowplow OY, which occasionally runs for photographers and to clear the line at the end of winter. Jeff Mast was part of a group who photographed its operation near Cresco on March 1, 2020.

Yellow aspens light up the Toltec Gorge in the fall of 2021 as Rio Grande Southern locomotive 20, visiting the Cumbres & Toltec from the Colorado Railroad Museum, leads a "photo freight" west during a charter organized by Pete Lerro. This location, while relatively unchanged from the Rio Grande days, was rarely seen in photographs from that era due to its remoteness. Photographer William Diehl (an engineer for Amtrak) notes that crushed ballast now predominates on the railroad, which is a significant improvement over the D&RGW's maintenance practices.

Cumbres & Toltec 168—a 4-6-0 locomotive built in 1883 for the Denver & Rio Grande—leads a passenger train out of Antonito at sunrise in a William Diehl photograph from a Pete Lerro charter trip in 2021. During the latter years of Rio Grande operations, trains running anywhere on the narrow gauge at sunrise were rare, as most crews were called to start work in the midmorning. Special trains like this one have opened up new opportunities for photography.

The sun has set on Cumbres Pass as October 24, 2022, draws to a close and the *Toltec Rattler*, a photo freight charter, prepares to return to Chama near the end of an all-day round-trip to Big Horn. While the train harks back to the freights of more than half a century earlier, Nicholas D'Amato used the full spectrum of modern digital photography to create a color image that would have been impossible to obtain in the Rio Grande era. The sensor of his digital camera has many times more light-gathering ability and exposure latitude than any color film available in the 1960s. He also used the digital darkroom to remove two modern vehicles parked to the left of the train. D'Amato—like his brother, Anthony, as well as Justin Franz and William Diehl, whose photographs also appear in this section—was born many years after the last Rio Grande freight trains ran in 1968. These photographers are living proof that the narrow gauge is as compelling as ever, and that there is still no cure for anyone exposed to its wonders.

AFTERWORD

Richard Tower

Board of Directors

Center for Railroad
Photography & Art

IT'S BEEN FIFTY-FIVE YEARS since Denver & Rio Grande Western freight trains last ran on the San Juan Extension, but in many ways remarkably little has changed. The same narrow-gauge Mikados are still dispatched from Durango, Chama, and Antonito. Durango has grown, but other lineside communities are still a part of small-town, rural America. Particularly on the Cumbres & Toltec, members of families who settled the area when it was still Spanish and Mexican territory continue to work for the railroad. Surnames such as Martinez, Pacheco, and Ulibarri have filled the employment rolls for generations. And the great rocky peaks, the lovely green valleys, and the swift mountain streams are as picturesque as ever.

But some things are different. The business of the railroads is carrying passengers now. While the D&RGW as a freight hauler was important to the local economy, the successor roads Durango & Silverton and Cumbres & Toltec Scenic have an even larger impact. More than 200,000 visitors ride the trains each year and provide significant support to local businesses. Economic success no longer depends on the needs of the Farmington oil fields or the number of sheep to be moved each fall. Factors such as the price of gas and family decisions on how to spend vacation time now affect the railroads' bottom lines.

In recent years there have been challenges, both financially and operationally. Anchored by the large commercial and tourist town of Durango at one end and the historic mining community of Silverton at the other, the D&S usually carries about five times as many passengers as the C&TS. In normal years, its fare revenues fully support both the operating and capital costs of the railroad. While the C&TS covers its train operating costs from fare revenues, much of the capital expenses, including track rehabilitation and heavy locomotive overhauls, are covered by annual grants from the states of Colorado and New Mexico.

As always, nature continues to challenge the railroads. In D&RGW days, snow and washouts would halt operations, sometimes for weeks. But warmer and drier weather has now made fire a major risk. Both the D&S and the C&TS have been forced to temporarily halt service because of extreme dry conditions or the actual presence of wildland fire. Coal-fired locomotives bring the risk of sparks and cinders, and the railroads are now forced to make major expenditures for fire safety and prevention. Both railroads have converted some steam locomotives to burn oil, and the D&S has purchased diesel locomotives to substitute for steam in times of extreme fire danger.

Financial and operational challenges are nothing new to the narrow gauge. Both the C&TS and the D&S have shown they have the will and the resources to survive—and more. Particularly on the C&TS, the installation of thousands of crossties, reclaimed and resized from use on Class I carriers, and thousands of tons of crushed-rock ballast have put track in better shape than ever. Skilled shop workers on both railroads continue

to rebuild working locomotives and return to service locomotives that have lain unused for many years. Both railroads construct new passenger cars to fill the need for premium accommodations that many of their customers now desire. Three active volunteer groups—the Friends of the Cumbres & Toltec Scenic Railroad, the Durango Railroad Historical Society, and the Galloping Goose Historical Society—are rebuilding and maintaining rolling stock and buildings that help elevate the two railroads to the status of operating museums.

The Galloping Goose Historical Society lovingly maintains Rio Grande Southern Motor 5, which operates on the D&S and C&TS every year to sold-out crowds as a reminder of the improvised bus-on-rail-wheels that helped that carrier survive the Great Depression. The Durango Railroad Historical Society has rebuilt and maintains the 1895 Consolidation-type locomotive 315, originally owned by the Florence & Cripple Creek Railroad

and now operating on the C&TS. The Durango society is also restoring vintage freight cars at its shop facility in Silverton. And the Friends of the C&TS, active for many years with more than two thousand members, has restored a locomotive, dozens of vintage freight cars, passenger cars, and many lineside buildings. Not to be outdone, the C&TS Railroad itself, with funds from the State of Colorado and the Colorado State Historical Fund, has restored to service 1883 locomotive 168 and several nineteenth-century passenger cars.

What does this mean? Photographers made their way to southern Colorado and northern New Mexico decades ago to capture a unique and scenic railroad operation that might disappear at any time. Hopefully, the threat of disappearance is no longer a motivation. But the dramatic scenery and clear mountain air are still there. The trains are still running, and now there's more variety than ever. The photographers will keep coming.

Photographer William Diehl calls this image "Little Train to Oblivion," and it shows Cumbres & Toltec 463 leading a short photo freight out of Antonito at dawn in 2014, steaming west toward the cloud-strewn horizon. Bighorn Peak looms at right.

INDEX

Index of photographers

ACKNOWLEDGMENTS

THE INSPIRATION FOR this book came from John Mellowes and Rich and Caroline Tower. They are deeply devoted to the narrow gauge; John has built a world-class model railroad based on it in his basement, while Rich and Caroline are active in the Friends of the Cumbres & Toltec Scenic Railroad. They are also some of our most steadfast and generous supporters at the Center for Railroad Photography & Art. Looking for meaningful ways to thank them sent me into our collections in search of photographs of the narrow gauge, where the notion dawned on me that we have more than enough material for an outstanding book.

That we have these images is because the photographers took them in the first place, often expending great time, energy, and money to do so. They are listed in the index on the facing page, and they have our profound gratitude both for creating these photographs and for trusting us to preserve and present them. Great thanks, too, go to their spouses and other traveling companions, who did everything from tagging along to driving pacing vehicles. They include Kate Botkin, Roger Cook, Betty Gildersleeve, Sandra Hofsommer, Don Phillips, Gordon and Gail Roth, Carol Shaughnessy, Dale Springer, Nona Steinheimer, and Laurel Zimmermann. Additional recognition goes to Shirley Burman Steinheimer and Bonnie Gruber for their remarkable efforts to help preserve their late husbands' photography.

That we can share these photographs is thanks to the efforts of our team of archivists and interns at the Center. They are led by Adrienne Evans, and others who helped preserve and digitize the collections that appear in this book include Abigail Guidry, Natalie Krecek, Colleen O'Keefe, Jordan Radke, Erin Rose, Heather Sonntag, and John Walker.

Simona Jansons Gheorghiu at Asia Pacific Offset shepherded every aspect of this book's production with grace and patience, while the sales and marketing team at Baker & Taylor championed its distribution.

The Rio Grande narrow-gauge lines remain popular in all forms of media. The late Lloyd Stagner wrote a book with the same title, covering both narrow- and standard-gauge steam and published by South Platte Press in 1999. Several websites provided invaluable information to my research. I extend my gratitude to Nathan Holmes and his excellent drgw.net site, John West and his outstanding photography and captions on his chasingtrains.smugmug.com site, and everyone who posts on the Narrow Gauge Discussion Forum at ngdiscussion.net, a site whose collective depth of knowledge about the narrow gauge truly knows no limits.

The narrow-gauge railroaders, both past and present, deserve great thanks for making the trains run and also for so frequently making photographers welcome. That very much includes everyone at the current narrow-gauge railroads and their broader preservation community, in particular Paul Hammond and the rest of the outstanding staff and volunteers at the Colorado Railroad Museum for their eagerness to partner with us. Chuck Albi, a member of that superb organization as well as the Center, is a great champion for both institutions and an ongoing source of inspiration.

Many more members of our community stepped up to help. Board members Ron Batory, Jeff Brouws, Norman Carlson, Betsy Fahlman, Justin Franz, Roger Grant, Todd Halamka, Nona Hill, David Kahler, Kevin Keefe, Al Louer, Peter Mosse, and Michael Schmidt offered everything from conceptual ideas to proofreading to encouragement. Elrond Lawrence answered my call to assist as co-editor as well as with marketing and promotional efforts. David Styffe eagerly and expertly took on the map. Jim Armstrong graciously volunteered to assist with copyediting. Hailey Paige and Inga Velten threw their outreach energies and ideas behind this book in everything from online programming to thank you letters. With so much assistance and so many resources at my fingertips, I take full responsibility for any mistakes I introduced and that made it into print.

My late grandparents, Walter and Mary Frame, took me for my first ride on the narrow gauge, a winter trip to Cascade on the Durango & Silverton, while helping me move cross-country from Ohio for a college internship in Arizona. My wife, Maureen Muldoon, joined me for my most recent visit to the narrow gauge and offered her unending support, patience, and encouragement through the many evenings and weekends I spent on the image selection and preparation, research, writing, and editing involved in this project.

Finally, none of our efforts at the Center for Railroad Photography & Art would be possible without the remarkable support of our community of members and our board of directors. They empower everything we do. Bon French, who chairs our board, exemplifies their efforts and the very notion of volunteer leadership through his profound gifts of time, talent, and treasure. They are truly transformational.

—Scott Lothes, Madison, Wisconsin, 2023

Rio Grande Steam Finale: Narrow Gauge Railroad Photography in Colorado and New Mexico
Copyright © 2023
Center for Railroad Photography & Art
www.railphoto-art.org

"There is no cure"
© 2023, Don L. Hofsommer

"How I learned to love (and lose) the narrow gauge"
© 2023, Karl Zimmermann

All rights reserved
Printed in China
First edition

Book design and composition:
Scott Lothes

Front endpaper map design:
David Styffe

Rear endpaper photograph:
Victor Hand, passenger special east at Romeo, Colorado, on October 3, 1965

ISBN 978-1-7345635-2-8

ABOUT THE CRP&A

FOUNDED IN 1997, the Center for Railroad Photography & Art (CRP&A) is a 501(c)(3) national not-for-profit arts and educational organization based in Madison, Wisconsin. As its mission the CRP&A "preserves and presents significant images of railroading," securing them in its archive and interpreting them in publications, exhibitions, and on the internet.

The CRP&A conducts its programs both in-house and with numerous partners throughout the country. Collaborations include the landmark Chicago History Museum exhibition, *Railroaders: Jack Delano's Homefront Photography*, and 2019's *After Promontory: 150 Years of Transcontinental Railroading*, which has visited a dozen venues throughout the western United States, including the Brigham Young University Museum of Art. The CRP&A also mounts and circulates traveling exhibitions about specific themes in railroading as well as individual photographers and artists such as Wallace W. Abbey, Joel Jensen, David Plowden, Ted Rose, and Jim Shaughnessy.

Efforts to preserve railroad photography and artwork have led to the CRP&A's amassing more than 500,000 images—with standing commitments for that many more to come. Its professional archives team preserves, digitizes, and makes available these images from its offices and storage facilities, sharing them through an online database and social media (follow @railphotoart on all the major platforms). A committee of the board of directors reviews and makes recommendations to the full board for all potential additions to the archive.

In addition to books, the CRP&A publishes a quarterly journal, *Railroad Heritage*, featuring work by historic and contemporary photographers and artists. Events include an annual awards program, free monthly online presentations, and an annual conference where artists, historians, editors, and railroaders discuss their work and address artistic and photographic issues. Membership supports all of the CPR&A's programs and projects; learn more and join at: www.railphoto-art.org